To Bea
with best wishes

R.C.Kensett

A Walk in the Valley

Robert C. Kensett

Grishow 2004

Published by

GSPH GENERAL STORE
      PUBLISHING HOUSE

Box 28, 1694B Burnstown Road
Burnstown, Ontario, Canada K0J 1G0
Telephone (613) 432-7697 or 1-800-465-6072

ISBN 1-894263--76-6
Printed and bound in Canada

Design and layout by Leanne Enright
Cover design by Taragraphics
Printing by Custom Printers of Renfrew Ltd.

Copyright © 2003
General Store Publishing House
Burnstown, Ontario, Canada

Canadian Cataloguing in Publication Data

Kensett, Robert C., 1924-
        A walk in the valley / Robert C. Kensett.
ISBN 1-894263-76-6

        1. Kensett, Robert C., 1924- 2. Canada. Royal Canadian Air
Force–Biography. 3. World War, 1939-1945–Aerial operations, Canadian.
4. World War, 1939-1945–Personal narratives, Canadian.
5. Flight navigators–Canada–Biography. I. Title.

D811.K443 2002   940.54'4971'092   C2002-904884-2

"Yea, though I walk through the valley
of the shadow of death, I will
fear no evil:
for Thou art with me . . ."

From the 23rd Psalm

*FOR
MADELYN,
WHO WAITED FOR THE RETURN OF
A HUSBAND-TO-BE
OR PERHAPS
JUST A MEMORY*

PROLOGUE

My paternal grandmother, Charlotte, or Lottie, as she was called by friends, told fairy stories. I had better explain that. She was born into a humble family living in Windsor, Berkshire, England. The huge Windsor Castle loomed over the town and during her childhood and into her teens she must have seen royalty coming and going, heard music coming from the walls as great balls were held, and been witness to all the pomp and pageantry, and she was greatly impressed.

To go back a few years. Charlotte's paternal grandmother, Jane, on becoming a widow, cleaned other peoples' houses to earn enough to provide for her family. She was a charwoman. Jane's son William, at the age of seventeen, was an errand boy and in later life his occupation was listed as "groom." Jane's daughter, Dorothy, was a live-in maid and then a seamstress. So Charlotte's family, the Waymans, were honest, simple people with no pretensions of grandeur.

In due course Charlotte married a soldier, William Kensett, a private in the regular army. After a stint in Windsor he was transferred to the Tower of London, where they lived in the married quarters and where their first son, William, was born. I believe it was about this time that Charlotte decided that if she could not actually live a life in the higher circles she would invent one; and at this point, to put it kindly, she began to tell her fairy stories, which hurt no one but in fact were rather large fibs.

As the years passed, these stories were told over and over by her children, their spouses, and so on, down to the grandchildren. They became part of the family history, accepted by all. Of course they could not be about the Kensetts, since her husband would realize they were not true, so they were all about *her* family, the Waymans.

She said that her father, the groom, had been employed at Windsor Castle to train the Windsor grey horses that were used on state occasions. These assertions were backed up by little stories that made them believable. One my mother told me many times. Once, when Queen Victoria was walking around the coach and got very close to the horses' heels, William Wayman said, "For God's sake, Madame, be careful!" An aide said, "Wayman, you cannot talk to the Queen that way," to which the Queen replied, "William was only doing his duty."

After leaving the army, William Kensett was employed as a porter in Paddington Station, London. That provided grandmother with another scenario, and so one of her ancestors became outrider to the Queen, taking the train ahead of her own to ensure the track was clear and all was in readiness for her stop at some destination down the line. A very important job indeed.

My father was born in the district of Paddington, although grandmother always said he was born in Wimbledon, a much more fashionable district. My father was named Robert Charles after two uncles, and so escaped the Wayman name, which grandmother perpetuated every chance she could. Her other sons were William Wayman, John Wayman, and Arthur Wayman; and even my sister is Joan Wayman. I have cousins with the middle name of Wayman, so grandmother managed to keep the name going through a couple of generations.

Along with grandmother's stories it was impressed upon us that the British Empire was "something else," and serving King and country was the noblest of professions. She impressed her four sons so much that all enlisted in World War I.

One son returned home unscarred. One son was a prisoner of war for three years. My father, after a mere three months at the front, was sent on a night patrol in no man's land with his younger brother; a shell knocked my father unconscious and, on coming to, he found himself badly wounded and his brother lying dead beside him. He had to crawl away in the mud back to his own lines, leaving his brother behind. Still, after such an experience, when I was a small boy my father continued marching in his kilts to the skirl of the pipes, and we watched the parades with pride.

Early in 1939, one of my older cousins did not wait for Canada to become involved in World War II; he went to England and joined the RAF. That established his status as Grandmother's favourite grandchild and he became a hero to the family. He was a rear gunner stationed in North Africa, and miraculously survived the war. What part Charlotte's stories played in his decision to enlist we can only speculate upon, but he was a harum-scarum kind of fellow and no doubt the glamour of the air force appealed to him.

In 1923, everyone was in Canada; Grandmother decreed that the family should return to England, whence they had come. The women would go first and the men would follow. At that time Charlotte ruled the family with an iron fist and no one dared to disobey her. However, Charlotte changed her mind and sent everyone back to Canada. My mother went to her parents' home and found out she was carrying me; so when the order came from Grandmother to return to Canada my mother stayed behind.

"The Teller of Fairytales": My paternal grandmother, Charlotte, whose fibs and stories pushed me along to my enlistment. For some unknown reason, she is wearing my father's hat!

Author

The King's Arms Inn. Copy of an etching of the pub run by my grandfather, James Sartin. The inn was located at a crossroads in the hamlet of Hilperton's Marsh. The etching was done from a photograph by my stepdaughter, a talented graphics artist. Barbara could not resist a few touches of her own: a cat is looking out of the upper window on the left in the room in which I was born, in 1924.

Artist: Barbara Wood

On February 20th, 1924, I was born in an upstairs room of the King's Arms Inn, a pub owned by my grandfather, William Sartin. The pub was located in Hilperton's Marsh, which was just outside of Hilperton, which was just outside of Holt, which was just outside of Trowbridge. It was indeed a small hamlet!

It was only a few years ago when researching the family tree that I uncovered Grandmother's fibs. None of the glorious occupations she had ascribed to her family actually existed. However, while growing up I did not know this, so I was imbued with a strong sense of duty. Also, my mother had trained me to believe that men looked after their womenfolk; and as my father had died when I was nine, there was only me to protect my mother, my sister, and my girlfriend Madelyn. In Canada the draft was in effect and I certainly did not want to suffer the life my father had

James and Lavinia Sartin, my maternal grand-parents. James was a plasterer by trade and then became landlord of the King's Arms Inn. Lavinia bore thirteen children, and had to count them on her fingers when recalling all of their names for the visiting rector!

Author

endured in the army, consisting of mud, lice, and hand-to-hand combat. Having been born in England, and considering my upbringing, is it any wonder, then, that soon after my eighteenth birthday I presented myself at an RCAF recruiting centre?

Of all the tales told by my grandmother one was in fact true. Queen Victoria's consort, Albert, had established the Royal Association "for improving the condition of labourers and others." The association awarded prizes for various accomplishments, and Jane Wayman, my great, great grandmother, won a prize of one pound in 1862, for "cleanliness and tidiness in house and person." As I write this I can look at the framed certificate on the wall of my den. At least one member of the Wayman family achieved a measure of fame. Considering living conditions in 1862 it was perhaps not as modest an accomplishment as at first it might seem!

James and Lavinia Sartin, my maternal grand-parents. James was a plasterer by trade and then became landlord of the King's Arms Inn. Lavinia bore thirteen children, and had to count them on her fingers when recalling all of their names for the visiting rector!

Author

endured in the army, consisting of mud, lice, and hand-to-hand combat. Having been born in England, and considering my upbringing, is it any wonder, then, that soon after my eighteenth birthday I presented myself at an RCAF recruiting centre?

Of all the tales told by my grandmother one was in fact true. Queen Victoria's consort, Albert, had established the Royal Association "for improving the condition of labourers and others." The association awarded prizes for various accomplishments, and Jane Wayman, my great, great grandmother, won a prize of one pound in 1862, for "cleanliness and tidiness in house and person." As I write this I can look at the framed certificate on the wall of my den. At least one member of the Wayman family achieved a measure of fame. Considering living conditions in 1862 it was perhaps not as modest an accomplishment as at first it might seem!

CHAPTER 1

FIRST INTERVIEW

Several young men were sitting in a waiting room and I joined them. I was given a sheet of paper with numerous questions, which I held on my knee and filled out with a pencil I had borrowed from a sergeant sitting at a desk beside a door to another room. One by one, the men were called by the sergeant, who escorted them into the other room. Finally it was my turn and I found myself sitting across from an officer of the RCAF. He asked me why I had chosen the air force, and I told him about my father's terrible experiences in the army in World War I and about my cousin in the RAF. He never asked about the navy, and I was spared the embarrassment of telling him I could not swim!

He had the form I had filled out in front of him and noted that I had put down aircrew rather than ground crew or administration. He then asked me what I thought I would like to be and I immediately replied "air gunner." I explained that it was my understanding that this was the most hazardous position in the crew, and therefore that's what I wanted to do. He had the good grace not to smile; and without a change in his expression he suggested I wait until I had some training, after which I would know for which post I was best suited.

He ended the interview by telling me I would be notified later as to when and where to report. I thought things had gone quite well, even if I had been very nervous, and I left knowing that the first step had been taken. I believed that I was well on the way to serving King and Country. Little did I know what a hard and long road lay ahead!

MEDICAL

Before I could be sworn in I had to pass a medical exam. There was the usual poking and probing, and then the doctor administered two tests that I almost did not pass. The first involved balance, and consisted of standing on one foot and then closing my eyes. I am not sure how many seconds one had to hold this pose, but I had to put the other foot down or fall over in a very few seconds. The doctor gave me a second chance, and I am sure he let me off with fewer seconds than were required. He said time was up just before my other foot hit the floor. Apparently there were not going to be many instances in the air force where you had to stand on one foot with your eyes closed!

The second test involved sitting in front of a gadget that had a column of mercury in it. By blowing into a mouthpiece you could move the mercury up the column and you were supposed to keep it above a certain level for a certain length of time. This was to test the strength and capacity of your lungs. I took a deep breath and blew but it was not very long before I had to breathe again, and down came the column of mercury. The doctor was very understanding and let me rest a while. Then he told me to relax and when I was ready to try again. He was sitting beside me and he took one of my hands in his and held it to reassure me. Once more I took a deep breath and blew. This time I was determined to keep that column of mercury up the tube, and I kept the pressure up until my lungs were bursting and my chest was starting to heave looking for oxygen. Finally I had to stop and gasp for air. I found I was still holding the doctor's hand, and I had squeezed it until his fingers were white! I passed—but I am sure it was several minutes before the doctor got any feeling back into his fingers!

I did not see the comments appended to my medical report until I began to assemble material for this book. If I had seen them then I would have been crushed. They said:

> Immature. Introverted. Shy but rather calm. Likes to work with figures. Unable to drive a car. Has no mechanical interests. Overseas OK. No family objections. Not very impressive but looks best as Bombardier.

Not the assessment for which one would wish, but nevertheless I must agree it was accurate at the time.

MANNING POOL

I had a few anxious months of waiting, but finally came word to report to Manning Pool, which was located in the Exhibition Grounds in Toronto. There I was sworn in, on February 3rd, 1943, and over the next day or two I was issued a uniform, my picture was taken and an ID card given to me. Martha's boy, Robert Charles Kensett, had been magically transformed into R219756, an aircraftsman second class in his Majesty's Royal Canadian Air Force.

For the first ten days we were in quarantine and were housed in what had been the sheep pens. At least once a day we were herded into an enclosed area to be harangued by a warrant officer standing on a balcony. His job, or so it appeared to be, was to frighten us— which he was able to do quite easily. I can only recall one of his favourite admonitions and that was, if we did anything wrong "I'll piss on you from great heights and I always have a bellyful!"

We were given a number of injections to test our immunity to certain diseases. Unfortunately I failed them all and so received a total of nineteen shots in the ten days. We lined up in single file to pass between two doctors, each of whom delivered a shot for one disease or another. When I arrived, a sergeant called out my name and number and said, "Hands on your hips, a great big smile," and the two doctors plunged a needle into each of my arms!

Finally our period of quarantine was over and we were able to go home for an hour or two once in a while. Our family and friends were able to admire our uniform, even though we were the lowest of the low. This was brought to my attention quite forcibly one day when I was walking through Manning Pool, and coming toward me was a wing commander with whom I had had several conversations as a bank teller a few months previously. I gave him my smartest salute with a broad smile. He returned the salute with the stoniest of stares, his eyes boring right through me. Obviously the relationship between a wing commander and an AC2 was quite different from that of a wing commander and a bank teller!

The atmosphere in Manning Pool was something else. Animal odours still exuded from the walls and floors, and that, coupled with the smell of cabbage cooking, and the fact that hundreds of men inhabited a small space, all contributed to the pungent air. Almost everyone developed a hacking cough, but the canteen sold a wondrous cough syrup that tasted like thick prune juice and amazingly soothed the throat. We sat on benches at long tables where we ate cabbage meal after meal. A hot beverage was placed on the table in a large pitcher. After tasting, a vote was held that was split about 50/50 between tea and coffee. We never did find out what it was.

I shared a double bunk bed with Conrad Eidt, a farm boy from Owen Sound, and we became fast friends, managing to stay together for a couple of years. He was very quiet and never swore, and I think we recognized in each other a kindred spirit. Most of our days were spent outside learning the intricacies of proper drill, for which the same sergeant shouted at us every day. On our last night he came around and had a few drinks with some of the fellows. This was of course strictly forbidden, but you gained the impression he had done this many times before!

Robert C. Kensett. Aircraftsman Second Class R
219756. Newly enlisted. Age eighteen and scared stiff.
Author

At any time during the day the loudspeakers would blare out "God Save the King." Woe betide those who did not snap to attention at the first notes. Sometimes the anthem would not be played for a number of hours and at other times only ten minutes would elapse before they tried to catch you napping.

At last our sojourn at Manning Pool came to an end and we were transferred to Camp Borden. This was a training station for pilots, but of course this was not for us. We were given joe jobs, which, if nothing else, taught us humility.

CHAPTER 2

CAMP BORDEN

We arrived in Camp Borden on March 25th. The pilots in training were using Harvard trainers, which must have been the noisiest aircraft ever built. Flying took place night and day and there was no escaping the roar of the engines. Mercifully you eventually learned to live with it.

The food at Camp Borden was much better than at Manning Pool. There was one added attraction, a doughnut-making machine. We soon learned to stuff our pockets with doughnuts. After all we were just growing boys and always had a space to be filled. As I only weighed 127 pounds I must have had a lot of space available!

I spent my first day washing an aircraft with a small cloth and a pail of water, which job did not strike me as much of a contribution to the war effort. Worse was to come. Some of us were detailed to carry out night guard duty. This entailed climbing a ladder into a tower on the perimeter of the station, and spending the night sitting on a plank and looking for intruders. We were even armed. We were given .303 rifles. However, we were given only one bullet and that was to be kept in the breast pocket of our battledress. As we were wearing scarves and greatcoats, it being winter, the bullet was further hidden. In the event of an emergency you could not imagine yourself shouting, "Halt while I find my bullet!" We had two hours on and two hours off with a meal in the middle of the night. I spent my time dreaming of Madelyn and trying to compose poetry for her without success.

After my stint on guard duty I was told to report to the control tower. I sat on a bench trying to keep my eyes open, and finally I was told to go to a small truck parked at the end of a runway. The trainee pilots were practicing takeoffs and landings, more descriptively known as circuits and bumps, and an officer beside the truck told me what he was doing. When a pilot came in to land, if no one was near him, you shone a green Aldis lamp at him. If two planes were going to land and were too close to each other you shone a red Aldis lamp at the second plane, which told him to go round the circuit again. If there were numerous planes approaching at the same time you fired off a red Very pistol, and that meant they were to scatter to avoid hitting each other. After I had been watching for a while, he said he had to go to the control tower and that I should carry on. I gave red and green lamps to quite a few pilots before he returned, but fortunately never had to reach for the Very pistol. I wondered what the pilots would have thought had they known their lives depended on an AC2 who had had five minutes' instruction.

One night one of the pilots turned the wrong way in the circuit. He must have panicked when he saw the other planes coming straight at him. He dove to get out of the way but was too low and went straight into the ground. The next day we all trooped over to look at the huge hole. This was our first experience with death, but I can't say it bothered us much. We did not know the fellow and had not seen the accident occur. Still, it did serve to remind us that being in aircrew was indeed hazardous.

OTTAWA

Our next stop was Ottawa, where we took a pre-aircrew education course. The course was taught by teachers at the Ottawa Technical High School and, as these teachers were busy all day, we attended classes in the evenings. There were only three subjects and they were so simple no studying was required. We accordingly had a great deal of time on our hands and were able to go sightseeing and generally relax. There were no parades or drills and the change to indolence was welcome.

We were housed in groups of five or six in boarding houses within walking distance of the school and the downtown area. I had a bedroom on the second floor and we all met in a large dining room for our meals. The lady who ran the rooming house was a pleasant, middle-aged woman, and she was a cheerful person so we enjoyed our stay. We had so much time on our hands that we started a contest to see who could have the shiniest shoes!

One Saturday night Con and I treated ourselves to dinner in the famous Chateau Laurier hotel. We went to the main dining room and shortly after we were seated, an elderly couple was placed at the next table. The gentleman ordered a bottle of wine and all through the meal their glasses were topped up by the waiter. Up to that stage of my life I had only had a sip or two of wine at Christmas, or perhaps a taste of the stout my mother bought once in a while. I was fascinated by the slowly emptying bottle and could hardly believe they drank it all. Then they stood up and walked away quite sober! Amazing!

At the conclusion of the six-week course a Certificate of Education was issued stating that Robert C. Kensett had taken the Royal Canadian Air Force final exam in the following subjects and was recommended as educationally qualified for the category of Aircrew at an Initial Training School [ITS].

Subject	Mark
English	87
Science	100
Mathematics	100

Remarks: Keen. Neat. Intelligent.

This was certainly an improvement over the previous assessment, even if I still couldn't drive a car! But you had to remember that the instructor was a civilian, not an air force officer.

INITIAL TRAINING SCHOOL (ITS)

We always seemed to get sent from one place to another during the night and on the oldest trains. This move was no exception. I suppose the rail lines had less traffic at night. Some of the cars had no upholstered seats, simply wooden benches around the walls. They looked as though they might have been used in the Depression days of the '30s to move migrant workers out west.

The train clicked and clacked through Quebec's eastern townships, heading for Victoriaville, where the ITS was located. There we would learn the trade in aircrew for which we were best suited. It felt good that the preliminaries were over, but there was still a lot of work ahead. As yet I had never even been inside a plane, let alone up in the air!

The school used a complex of buildings that, until taken over by the government, had been a convent. When we arrived we were allotted our rooms and given the training schedule. We learned just how many subjects we would be expected to study. There were nine:

Aircraft Recognition
Armament
Principles of Flight
Engines
Law, Discipline, Administration and Organization
Mathematics
Meteorology
Navigation
Signals Buzzer
Signals Lamp

On top of the classroom work, every day brought an hour or two of drill on the parade square under the stern eye of a sergeant with a voice that certainly kept your attention!

We soon settled into the new routine. I found an organ in a loft in what had been the chapel, and found I could produce the most marvellous chords. It was easy to close my eyes and imagine I was in a great cathedral in Europe as the sound reverberated throughout the chapel.

Air force life was agreeing with me and I was getting fit by running three miles every day on an oval track beside the parade ground. As the buildings were of frame construction, there was a fire watch every night. We were well along in the course by the time it was my turn to wander the deserted halls, flashlight in hand, ensuring all was well. To pass the time I recited the parts of the machine gun to myself.

One day during our drill session the sergeant did not think we were as good as he thought we should be, and he had us back on the square after supper. We certainly smartened up for that session, as his temper was not of the best. Near the end, an AC2 came up to the sergeant and said that the CO (commanding officer) sent his compliments on the smartness of the flight. The CO's office was on the second floor and he had seen us going through our paces from his window. When the sergeant dismissed us I think we were all wearing smug smiles!

We learned to fire pistols, rifles and machine guns. One rule was drilled into us constantly: Always check to see if the gun is loaded. The instructor would try to catch you by asking for the gun and then handing it right back. Woe betide you if you didn't check to see if it was loaded. On the final exam we were told we would lose half of the marks if we did not do this, so that was one rule we never forgot.

Part of our training was on a "Link" trainer, a machine that simulated flight. Another fun subject was aircraft recognition, where slides were used to show images of different kinds of aircraft on a screen. You had to identify the aircraft, and toward the end of the course the image was only shown for about half a second! However, after the first lesson or two I knew that I wanted to be a navigator. The mathematics involved, the solving of problems and the log and chart keeping all appealed to my sense of order. My mind and heart were captured by this trade and I applied myself wholeheartedly.

Before the final exams we were interviewed by an officer who asked what we would like to do in aircrew. I didn't hesitate for a minute and said, "navigator." I had done well on the Link trainer and as almost everyone wanted to be a pilot he was surprised. He said, "We shall have to see how you do on the final exams."

The course ended on August 20th, 1943 and my grades were as follows:

Course	%
Aircraft Recognition	85
Armament	64
Engines	86
Principles of Flight	89
Law, Discipline, Admin. and Organization	85
Mathematics	89
Meteorology	84
Navigation	98
Signals Buzzer	100
Signals Lamp	100

One assessment we were not told at the time was under the heading of Character and Leadership, and I received 80% in that, a lot better than the first report I had received on enlisting, even if I still could not drive a car!

Having obtained 147 out of 150 marks in Navigation, resulting in a final 98%, I heard no more about becoming a pilot but found myself posted to the Air Observers School in Malton, Ontario, which was close to home. A number of the fellows were posted to the same school, including Con Eidt.

I have always wondered where I lost the three marks . . .

AIR OBSERVERS SCHOOL (AOS)

Those who passed the ITS course were promoted to leading aircraftsmen. Not much of a jump in rank, but better than being discharged! The insignia for this rank was an airplane propeller on each sleeve and a white flash in your forage cap. At least we were set apart from the lowly AC2s.

On September 5th, 1943, I arrived at Malton to train as a navigator on course #84. This would be my first training in the air, and so I was issued a logbook in which a record was kept of all flights in which I was involved. It followed me to the end of the war and I have it beside me now, a little the worse for wear after fifty-six years, but still a treasured memento.

A happy flyer who has yet to fly.
Mrs. Joan Wayman Donald

Joining the course were two or three fellows who had washed out of (failed) pilot training courses. One chap had wrecked three Tiger Moths, the training plane on his station. His last accident occurred when a sudden wind shift took the single-engine craft into a tall tree! He climbed out of the wreckage at the top of the tree and ignominiously made his way down to earth. He had salvaged a number of pieces of Plexiglas from the various planes he had wrecked, and from these he carved little hearts and other trinkets in his spare time. I think he was actually relieved that flying an aircraft was no longer his responsibility!

A day or two after our arrival, we were issued with flying suits and helmets. The next time I went into Toronto to see my mother and sister, I bundled up the suit and helmet and took them with me. I put them on so they could see what I looked like, and my sister and I went down into the back yard and she took my picture. Although I had yet to wear the outfit on a flight, I was proud to have even been issued with this gear.

* * *

Before the course began we had a day or two to settle in. We were told that anyone wanting an airplane ride should see the control tower. I had never been up in a plane before, so off I went to the control tower with my flying suit and helmet. I did not have long to wait, as an Anson was going on a training flight and I was sent out to the aircraft.

The Avro Anson was designed in England in the mid-1930s. Soon recognized by the Royal Air Force as a worthwhile aircraft, it was used, in 1936, on anti-submarine patrols. It soon became known as "Faithful Annie."

The Anson became the mainstay of Training Command and airframes and engines were manufactured in England and shipped to Canada for assembly. After 1940, England could no longer supply these parts in sufficient quantity, and five factories were set up in Canada. The Anson was used to train pilots and also to train other trades, and was the most widely used plane. Between 1941 and 1954, 4,431 Ansons were in use.

Specifications:

Wingspan	56 feet 6 inches
Length	42 feet 3 inches
Weight	7,663 lbs
Engines	300 hp
Speed	170 mph

In 1943 someone named Andy, in training at Fort MacLeod, penned the following:

> Oh the Crane[1] may fly much faster,
>
> Inside she may be neat
>
> But to me the draughty Anson
>
> Is very hard to beat.
>
> Her plywood may be warping,
>
> Her window glass may crack
>
> But when you start out in an Anson
>
> You know that you'll come back.

There was a small door back near the tail that the pilot, co-pilot and navigator, who was being trained, climbed in and I crawled in after them. The navigator sat at a table behind the pilot, but there was no other place to sit. I was told to sit down on the floor back by the door! There was nothing to hang on to, so I just braced myself with my hands on the floor. The roar of the twin engines seemed deafening to me, and the plane shook and shuddered. We tore down the runway, bouncing quite a bit, and then took off. I kept myself well braced, not knowing what would occur next. It was exciting to look out the little window in the door and see the earth come closer as we came in to land, and then feel the bump as we touched down. When the plane came to a halt and the engines were shut down I

---

[1] The Crane was another twin-engine training plane.

Course #84 at #1 AOS Malton. I am on the extreme right of the middle row, apparently a little more confident than when I enlisted, but still pretty serious! Conrad Eidt is fourth from the right in the back row. The corporal in front of me is an Englishman sent to Canada for his training in aircrew.

Author

climbed out on shaky legs with my ears still ringing, but I was happy that I had survived without becoming airsick!

Our own training finally got underway. At the beginning you flew as second navigator and watched what went on; but then you started acting as first navigator, doing all the plotting and giving courses to the pilot to get around the track they had laid out for you to follow on your chart.

All of the flights were in Ansons and the pilots were generally an unhappy bunch, as here they were, hauling navigators-in-training around instead of getting into the thick of the war. They distrusted the information we gave them and in some cases they probably had good reason. On one night flight, one navigator gave a reverse course to the pilot. They were flying above cloud and could see no landmarks; and when they finally got their bearings they had flown across Lake Ontario and were in the United States!

The smog in southern Ontario was terrible, and when there was an inversion—a situation where the air got warmer rather than cooler as you got higher—the terrible air was all trapped at lower altitudes and it looked so thick you thought you could have landed on it. On one such flight with no landmarks to be seen, the pilot was not content to rely on what I was telling him. He flew lower and lower and found a town with a water tower on which he could read the town's name. Satisfied that he knew where he was (we were where I said we were), he carried on. I had not learned how you plotted a circle on your chart, which is what he had flown around the water tower, so I dutifully recorded a square with sides about an eighth of an inch long on my chart. That must have passed muster, as I heard no complaints from the navigation officer.

We had learned a little about meteorology at ITS, and we continued this study at AOS. Ever since, I have been interested in weather patterns and always read the weather news and follow the charts in the newspapers. Cumulonimbus clouds were the most interesting, and you never flew into them, as the strong updrafts and downdrafts could break a plane apart in seconds.

We also studied aerial photography. Directing the pilot to the designated spot to be photographed was not dissimilar to the bomb-aimer's actions during a bombing run.

Astral navigation was also taught, and we soon learned how, with the aid of a sextant, to obtain a "cocked hat"—the triangle resulting from three position lines intersecting. A sextant is a hand-held instrument with mirrors and a graduated arc of 60° used to measure the altitude of heavenly bodies. Through one eyepiece you look through the two mirrors. One mirror is level with the horizon when a bubble is centred. The second mirror is rotated through the arc until a chosen star is centred; at which time, the bubble and star appear in the same spot. A reading is then taken from the arc, giving the star's altitude above the horizon and the exact time recorded. A book gives the altitude of stars at given times from different positions on the earth, and reference to tables in this book give you your position line for your chart. Three such calculations give you your cocked hat.

This was easy enough to do on the ground, but when in the air it was a different matter. The aircraft's movements made accurate readings very difficult. On my first crack at it, my cocked hat took in all of southern Ontario! It certainly did not give an accurate position of where we were; but if you stop and think about it, we were in fact inside of my cocked hat, as we had not had time to fly out of southern Ontario!

Our days were full, what with lectures in the classroom, flying on training flights, practising using the sextant and studying; but we still had the odd day off to get on the bus to Toronto, and I was able to see my mother and sister and Madelyn reasonably often.

* * *

One day we were shown how important *oxygen* was when you were flying. We were taken to a building that contained a large steel drum-like structure in the centre of the room. It was a decompression chamber. Eight of us entered a door at one end with an instructor and seated ourselves on benches that ran along each side. We were given clipboards and a pencil, and sheets of paper on which there were 100 sums. They were simple additions with only about four numbers in each problem. We were told to see how many we could do in a minute. I managed ninety-eight before the instructor said time was up.

Then the door was closed, the instructor donned a mask, and a pump started to withdraw air from the chamber. A dial at one end showed the equivalent height you were at as the air was withdrawn and the pressure dropped. At 10,000 feet the procedure was halted and we were again given sheets with 100 additions on each—again very simple problems. This time, in the minute allowed I only managed about half!

The pump was restarted and at 18,000 feet we stopped our ascent one more time. When the sheets were handed out I thought to myself, "What a stupid exercise this is. All these sums are so easy. I have all the time in the world." I looked around to see how the others were doing. All seemed to have their heads down, so I thought I might as well humour the instructor and start adding. When the instructor called "Time's up," I had completed only three! Oxygen masks were then handed out, which we put on, and we came back to reality from the euphoria we had experienced.

The instructor asked if anyone wanted to go higher and three fellows said they would. At 22,000 feet, one by one they slumped over. The instructor quickly put oxygen masks on them and in just a few seconds they came to. We did another set of additions wearing the oxygen masks and again they were easy and I finished most of them. Air was pumped back in slowly, but partway down my ears became blocked and they had to level off the descent and wait until I got them cleared. When you were *losing* pressure, air built up in your sinus cavities but had no problem escaping; it was a different story when the air was trying to get back in. As external pressure *increased*, the openings had a difficult time letting air in. This resulted in a great deal of pain in your upper cheeks below your eyes where the main sinus cavities were located. Eventually by vigorous nose blowing, yawning and swallowing, the passages were cleared and we were able to get back to ground level.

When flying, oxygen was used when you went above 8,000 feet. The pilot kept watch on the altimeter that registered the plane's altitude and when it became necessary he gave the order to hook up to your oxygen supply. You wore a facemask and two connections in the form of a wire and a narrow tube that ran from it. The wire was plugged into the intercom system and the tube was for your oxygen. You did not breathe quite as freely wearing the mask as you did without it, but there seemed to be little difference whether you were breathing ordinary air or oxygen. However, your lungs and brain knew otherwise!

* * *

In the event the enemy decided to drop bombs containing poisonous gas on Great Britain, everyone was issued with a gas mask. We were no exceptions, and just to make sure we understood how efficient they were in protecting us from noxious fumes, we were given a demonstration.

Twenty or thirty of us were marched into a Nissen hut that was empty. We were all lined up around the walls and then told to put on the gas masks that had been handed to us at the door. In the centre of the hut the instructor placed a tray and there seemed to be some kind of powder or substance in it, which he lit with a match. Soon we could see fumes rising from the burning material, but the air we were breathing through the mask stayed fresh. We were marched around the hut a couple of times and then told to break into a trot. Breathing through the mask was not as easy as without it, and we were soon labouring for air; at which point we were instructed to take off the masks. As soon as we did, our eyes and lungs were assailed by the tear gas that was being used for the demonstration.

We had to trot around the hut at least twice before being allowed out the door into the fresh air. I tried to hold my breath, which was probably not a good move, for when I could hold my breath no longer I was gasping for air and took in more of the gas than I otherwise would have. One final lope round the hut, and I was out the door, where I stood gasping for air, my lungs burning, my eyes closed and stinging, and with tears running down my face. I never doubted the efficacy of gas masks after that lesson. Actually, we were fortunate that they had used tear gas. My brother-in-law, who was in the army, had been given a similar demonstration; only on that occasion they used a gas that made you ill. He said it was most unpleasant, as he lost his breakfast and took some hours to recover.

* * *

At one point in the war, a ship was sunk and, because they could not climb ropes, a number of sailors drowned when a rescue ship came alongside. The air force was determined that we would not suffer the same fate!

We were taken to a gym where heavy ropes had been fastened to beams in the high ceiling and taught the technique for climbing. You put your hands up above your head and grasped the rope. Then you wound the rope once around your right leg and let it pass over your right instep. By placing your left foot over the rope you could squeeze it between your feet. You pulled yourself up with your arms while keeping the rope over the right instep with your left foot. Then you in effect stepped on the rope with your left foot. Surprisingly enough you could relax your grip with your hands and remain stationary on the rope. You then grasped the rope higher up and repeated the manoeuvre. After a few tries it proved to be very easy and there was something heady about climbing up the rope and sliding back down so easily. I'm afraid I was not a physical person, and most things you were supposed to be able to do of a physical nature I found very difficult. However, this was one exercise I enjoyed and I would have kept at it longer if I had been given the opportunity.

* * *

It was the middle of winter and the flights were desperately cold. You put on as many clothes as you could under your flying suit, but it was your fingers that grew stiff with cold when you most needed them to write in your log and work on your chart. If your hands were the least bit damp, the skin stuck to any metal object, including your sextant if you were using it, and I lost the odd patch of skin this way. Madelyn got me a pair of gloves without fingers and they were a big help.

Our last flight was a low-level flight—simply map-reading our way around a course. This was quite exciting, as it was also a change for the pilot, who usually suffered from boredom; low-level flying kept him on his toes. At the end of this exercise we were near Lake Simcoe, and in one section of the lake there were some ice fishing huts. The pilot said, "Watch this!" and flew down to a height of about fifteen feet above the ground. He roared over the huts, and

NAVIGATION COURSE

FOR

NAVIGATORS OR AIR BOMBERS

Held at *#1 AOS, RCAF Malton, Ont.*

From *6 Sept /43* To *28 Jan /44*

GROUND WORK			AIR WORK		
Subject	Marks Allotted	Marks Obtained	Subject	Marks Allotted	Marks Obtained
Air Nav.—Elements	200	158	Air Nav.—Day	400	306
Air Nav.—Theory	200	182	Air Nav.—Night	200	162
Air Nav.—Exercises	200	156	Log Keeping	200	179
Meteorology	100	82	Reconnaissance	100	81
Signals—Written	A 50	50	Photography	50	42
Signals—Practical	V 50	50	Met. Observations	50	45
Aircraft Recognition	50	43	Bombing		
Reconnaissance	50	39.25	Signals—Air Operating		
Photography	50	46	TOTAL	1000	815
Armament	50	40	%		81.5

FLYING TIMES ON COURSE

Type	Day	Night
Anson	71:50	28:45
TOTAL	71:50	28:45

TOTAL	1000	846.25
%		84.6

Passed / ~~Failed~~

REMARKS:

[signature]
for Chief Instructor

Results of final exams in course No. 84, No. 1 AOS, Malton.

Author

Three newly commissioned officers. I am in the middle, Con Eidt is on the right. Unfortunately I do not have the third gentleman's name, but he had a wonderful sense of humour and it had been a delight to be in training with him. The aircraft is an Anson, what else?

Author

from each one, men came pouring out onto the ice wondering what on earth was happening. They would have heard little until the roar suddenly blasted over their heads and they must have been frightened out of their wits. Needless to say that episode did not appear in my log . . .

The course was a tough one, but I loved navigation and studied hard. On the final exams I led the course, and yet my marks were not all that great, I thought: 84.6% for groundwork and 81.5% for airwork.

This photo of Madelyn was taken when I was overseas. She was twenty-two years old.

James Miller Donald

There was a parade in a hangar for the graduation exercise and I was called up first to receive my prize for leading the course. It was a silver cigarette case, a very nice prize, but I did not smoke! At the same time my navigator's wing was pinned on. Madelyn, my sister, and my mother were there to watch and I marched up as smartly as I could, almost bursting the buttons on my uniform I was so proud.

A list of all those who passed had been posted on the bulletin board and we were all promoted to the rank of sergeant. The day after that, another list was posted, and those who had received the best marks

My navigators' wing.

Author

My sister Joan and me. I was a leading aircraftsman and had not yet received my navigator's wing. I was nineteen and don't look quite as frightened as I did on Day One!

Author

were commissioned as officers. My name was there and I did not even have time to have the sergeant's stripes sewn on but wore them pinned to my tunic. I was given a clothing allowance of $100, found myself a tailor in Toronto, and bought a dress uniform, a battle-dress, a greatcoat and a cap, all wearing the insignia of a pilot officer. I could hardly wait for it to be finished so that I could wear it for Madelyn.

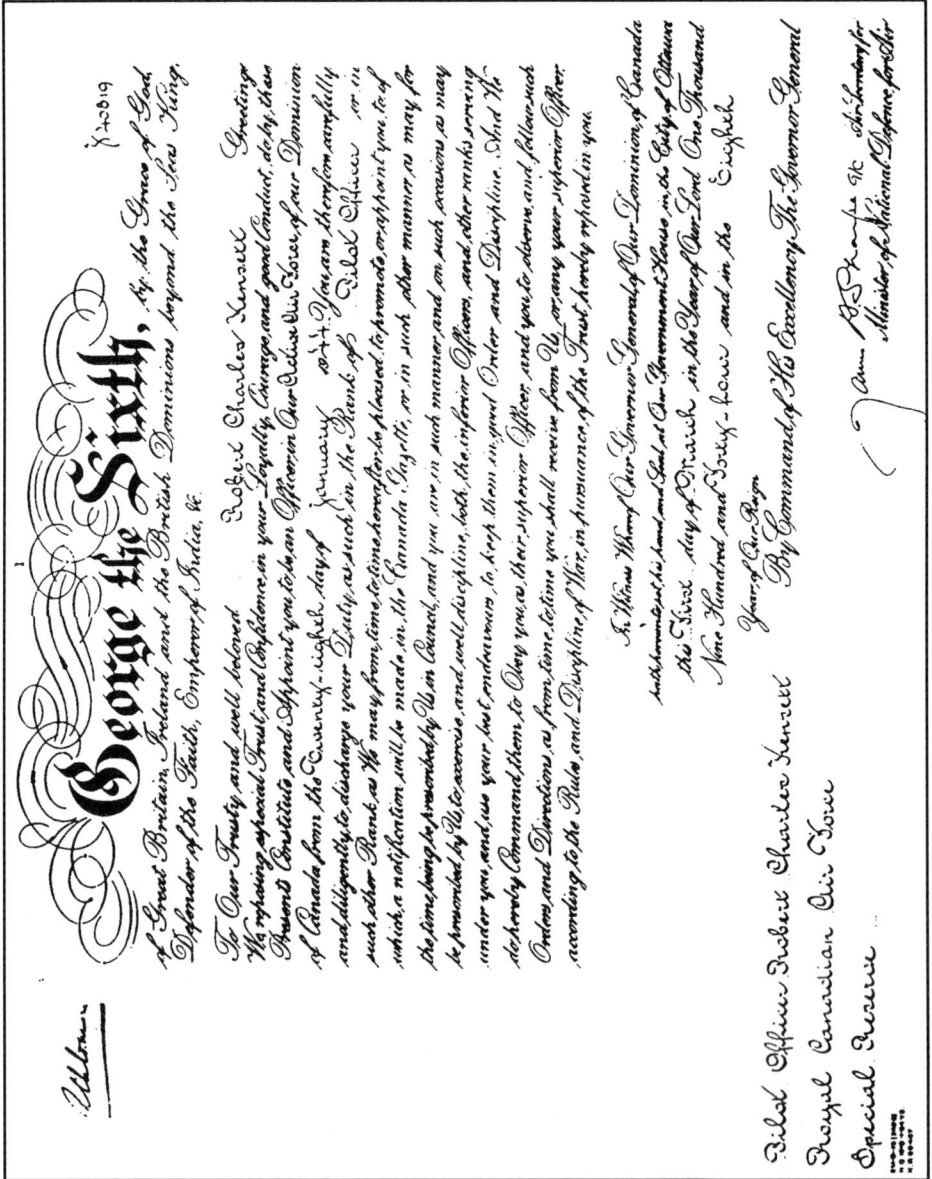

My commission as a pilot officer. The governor general's signature can be seen in the upper left-hand corner.

Author

Chapter 3

COMMANDO COURSE

After the AOS course ended, we were given leave—and what a wonderful interlude it was. I was able to be with Madelyn almost every evening. Although I was the world's worst dancer, I took her to Casa Loma where there was a full, live orchestra. We went outside for a stroll in the grounds. There was a full moon and suddenly, without a word, we turned to each other and kissed. That was almost sixty years ago but I can remember every second of that magical moment as though it were yesterday. I loved her dearly but did not want her married or engaged to someone who might come home a cripple—or perhaps not at all—so I never proposed. I don't think she was ready for a commitment at that time either.

Finally this wonderful holiday ended and I was posted to a commando course in Quebec City. There we were to be toughened in body and taught that we were officers and gentlemen. The latter consisted of a series of lectures on how to behave ourselves. We were told we should not consort with women. The talks were particularly gruesome at times, with slides of men in the final stages of venereal disease. Whether these slide shows and lectures had any effect on the other airmen I do not know, but they were unnecessary as far as I was concerned. It would seem that the brass doubted anyone was listening anyway, as the washrooms had boxes of condoms available for anyone who wanted them!

Our toughening-up routine consisted of forming up after breakfast and setting out on a route march that lasted until noon. We walked at quick march for ten minutes and then ran for ten minutes. Every hour we had a five-minute break. This was repeated in the afternoon. By the end of each session you felt you were at the end of your rope. However there was no way you would show your fatigue to any other flights on the station; so when you came within eyesight of the front gates you immediately started to run at double time until you were well within the station grounds.

We learned of the French Canadian's hatred of the war and conscription. Our route took us down many streets, and it was wintertime. Often we had snowballs thrown at us, some containing stones! We had to ignore these missiles and carry on as though nothing were happening. However, we were told not to roam the streets alone at night.

Near the end of the course, we were taken by trucks to a spot by the St. Lawrence River below the Plains of Abraham. This was where Wolfe and his army had scaled the cliffs to defeat the French. We were made to climb the steep cliffs not once, but twice in the course of a morning and we could appreciate how difficult it must have been, carrying rifles and packs, those many years ago.

ÎLE DE FRANCE

We were in Quebec City for roughly a month and then we were posted to Lachine, just outside of Montreal, to await transportation overseas. Each weekend found me heading home to Toronto to see my mother, Joan, and Madelyn. When the weekend was over, Joan and Madelyn would see me off at the railroad station. The first time or two we felt bad, but then it became a common occurrence; but sure enough, one weekend I did not turn up.

We boarded our train in Lachine in the evening and spent the night trying to sleep in the bunk beds with the train whistle sounding from time to time, the wheels continually clicking and clacking, and the railroad car swaying. However, before bedding down we had one of those wonderful meals that were then served on trains, with linen tablecloth and proper silverware. We had steaks (rare), a baked potato, peas, and apple pie with ice cream for dessert. There was no question that the beverage was real rich coffee. Little did we know what was coming.

The next morning found us on a siding beside the *Île de France*, a luxury liner that had been converted to a troop ship. We lined up on the dock with all our belongings, which we had to carry on board ourselves. Most of us had the same luggage: a trunk, a kitbag, and a rucksack over our shoulder. The gangplank was very steep. It had railings at both sides, but it was too narrow to hold your luggage beside you and you had to walk up with your arms extended over the railings holding your trunk and kitbag. It was all I could do to make it to the ship's deck, and my arms were aching when I reached the top. One poor chap couldn't manage it and dropped his trunk into the water when he was near the end of the harrowing journey. Everyone had to keep going, and I suppose he never recovered it before we sailed.

We were assigned our cabins. Everything had been stripped from the bulkheads inside, and double-decker bunks were lined up touching side by side. Our cabin had been a cabin for two, but there were seventeen of us crammed into it. A narrow passage went down the middle of the bunks, but this was obstructed by the rucksacks and coats hanging on the ends of the cots. You had to struggle between these and climb into your bed over the end! As it turned out I was the only one of our group who did not get seasick.

The ship had the speed to outrun submarines, and sped across the Atlantic on a zig-zag course at full speed. I don't know what was on the captain's mind but we never gave a thought to the possibility of being torpedoed and sunk.

We had two meals a day and our first was cold cereal with powdered milk and a kipper! I have hated kippers ever since. We soon learned to make jam sandwiches and put them in our pockets.

Once I tried to have a shower and that once was enough. The water was cold, salt water, and the soap produced no lather whatsoever. The Marquis de Sade would have been pleased. I should have realized right away what a disaster it was going to be, as I was the only one taking a shower in the huge room that contained dozens of showers.

We encountered no storms on the crossing; and day after day I stood at the rail on one of the higher decks, revelling in the sight of the spray reaching upward and the smell of the clean, salt air. The evening of our last day we rounded Northern Ireland and we could see the shoreline sliding past. The next morning when we came on deck we were anchored in the harbour at Greenock, Scotland. It is hard to express how I felt to be in the British Isles. My birth in England had been a quirk of fate and I had gone to Canada when I was just three months old. Many people would laugh at such feelings, but I felt in my heart that I had come home and I was overwhelmed.

We had a meal and then were taken ashore in cutters, each of which carried some fifty men. There were two pipers on the dock who piped us ashore. I was not a fan of the pipes but they did sound great at that moment with the sound coming across the water. It was a beautiful day with a bright blue sky and gulls wheeling overhead with their plaintive cries. The war seemed far away.

It took the whole day to get everyone ashore and onto a train. Once seated, we looked out to see a number of rather ragged-looking small boys, not more than eight or nine years old, with hands held out begging for cigarettes or chocolate bars. We suspected they were from the slums of Glasgow. Finally the train got underway, with all of the windows blacked out. After an hour or two someone came down the aisle and handed out tin plates and spoons. That fellow was followed by another pushing a trolley that held a large pot from which he ladled out a kind of stew onto your plate. This was supper and our introduction to wartime cuisine!

HOLDING STATION

We were on the train overnight and arrived at the holding station the next morning. It was located quite close to Churchdown, about midway between Gloucester and Cheltenham. Previously the holding station for new arrivals had been at Bournemouth on the south coast, but that area was now being used to build up the armies for the invasion—although we, of course, did not know this.

The billets were laid out in long rows, and between every two rows were laid out the showers, washrooms and toilet facilities. We had been there only a couple of days when one morning at 0630 hours, as we crossed over to the washrooms, we heard a growing roar; and then row after row of planes passed over at a very low altitude. As soon as one row had gone over, another appeared, and this went on for quite some time. It was the sixth of June, and we found out later in the papers about the D-Day landings in Normandy. The planes we had seen had been either carrying paratroopers or pulling gliders.

We spent several days at this station awaiting a posting to we knew not where. We were in the middle of a shallow valley and every so often during the day barrage balloons would be raised at each end. Then we would hear a high-pitched whining noise that completely baffled us. No one would tell us what was going on, but later we found out they had been testing fighter planes with jet engines. We never saw one take off or land. I suppose we were always looking in the direction of the whine, whereas the plane would have been far ahead of the noise due to its speed.

When a couple of days had passed someone decided there should be a parade, so we were all taken by trucks to a nearby airfield. When we arrived, the tailgate of the truck banged down and a British sergeant shouted at us, "Op to it, lads. Out you get!" In Canada it had been impressed on us that having received our commissions, we were officers and gentlemen. This order from a mere sergeant was not taken well. However, on getting out of the truck and looking around we saw that we were on a runway, and lined up as far as we could see were row upon row of officers and gentlemen! It was a humbling experience, as obviously in wartime Britain officers and gentlemen were a dime a dozen, especially if they were untried newcomers.

One morning I took the bus into Gloucester. On one street I saw a sign that said "milkshakes," and I went in and asked for one. The fellow behind the counter almost collapsed from laughter. He had not served a milkshake for years, as only powdered milk was available and ice cream was a forgotten memory. He said he could give me a lemon squash. I told him I would have one of those, expecting something like Orange Crush. He took a bottle that did not look too clean to me down from a shelf and measured a teaspoonful of some foul-looking liquid into a glass. He filled it up with tap water and gave it stir before sitting it in front of me. That was a lemon squash! It did taste a bit like lemon but it was warm, and of course not carbonated, and it was all I could do to get it down. Thankfully I don't remember what I paid for it!

* * *

On my first leave I caught the train to Trowbridge and stayed with my mother's sister, my Aunt Rose. Almost every leave I had thereafter I repeated these visits and I was probably one of very few airmen who did not go to London at some time during his stay in England.

My aunt and my Uncle Reg lived in what was called a council house. These were row houses built and owned by the town and they were leased to people with lower incomes. There was a back yard large enough for a garden, but the front yard was the size of a postage stamp, with a stone fence between it and the street. The street was narrow and the houses on the other side had no front yards at all, with only a narrow sidewalk separating the houses from the street. The street curved a few houses away from my aunt's and at the curve a laneway led to another street, which eventually brought you to downtown Trowbridge. The lane was bordered by the side of a house on one side and on the other by a high wall, the other side of which were grounds owned by the Church of England.

One feature of the house that was extremely odd to a Canadian was the fact that the toilet was located in a corner of the house, but could only be entered from the outside! You went out the kitchen door at the back of the house, past the coal bin, which was another room entered from the outside, and took a few steps to the door to the toilet, which was either called the water closet or the "loo." It got its name of "water closet" from the fact that the water was contained in a tank high up on the wall above your head. A long chain hung from the tank, and to flush the toilet you pulled on the chain.

A room with a washbasin and bathtub could be reached from the inside, and was just off the kitchen; the gas meter was located in this room. Before using hot water you always had to put a penny in the gas meter or you were liable to run out of hot water just when you needed it.

The kitchen was large enough for a table and chairs, and that was where meals were taken. At one side was a sink; during a visit in the winter I discovered that a drain ran from the sink through the kitchen wall and hung out over another drain in the ground leading to the town's storm drain system. I had been using the sink, and the water would not run away. When I traced the pipe outside there was a large icicle hanging from it, and this was blocking the water from splashing down into the drain in the ground. I suggested they affix the pipe from the sink to the drain in the ground and insulate it to prevent further blockages; but I was told it never got cold enough to make this necessary. Of course it did, and you were breaking off icicles almost every day. I soon learned that the English people resisted change with all their might. Many years later I read that the English resisted change, but when resistance eventually became futile they adopted the change wholeheartedly and acted as though they had invented the procedure!

There were three bedrooms upstairs each with a fireplace, but coal was scarce and these were never used unless someone was very ill and confined to bed. The living room on the main floor had a chesterfield and chairs grouped around the fireplace, and other pieces of furniture around the walls. It was small, but quite comfortable with a good fire going in the winter. There was no central heating and the bedrooms upstairs were cold. When it was bedtime everyone went out to the kitchen except the person going to bed first. That person got into pyjamas or nightie in front of the fire, called out he/she was going up, said goodnight, and then rushed upstairs and got into bed. I was always allowed to go first, followed by my cousin Beryl, and I'm sure my uncle was always last. If it was an extra cold night my aunt would heat up a brick on the stove, wrap it in a blanket, and put it in my bed so that when I crawled in it was nice and warm.

The radio was in the living room and my uncle Reg had his favourite programs that he always listened to each night. One was a comedy called Bleak House. One of the characters was an older man and every time someone would ask him something he would say, "I'll 'ave to ask me dad." You always knew he was going to say this, but my uncle would laugh every time it was said as though he were hearing it for the first time!

Uncle Reg had a skittles board and we would often have a game of skittles in the evening. The board was in the shape of a square about a foot across. On the board you set up pins that were about eight inches high. They covered the square with spaces between them and looked like the pins in a bowling alley, except they formed a square rather than a triangle. To the left was a post perhaps thirty inches high, and a piece of string was attached to the top of the post. At the end of the string a wooden ball was fastened. It was about an inch in diameter. The object was to take the ball in your hand and swing it out in the direction away from the pins. It would swing around in an arc and hit the pins on the way back to its starting point. You were given several turns, and whoever knocked down the most pins in this fashion won. A variation of the game that could be played by one person was to try and make the ball follow such arcs that the pins were knocked down one by one in a certain order; this was most difficult, unless of course you were Uncle Reg and had been playing for years.

My mother had several sisters living in and around Trowbridge, and Aunt Rose took me on the bus to meet them all so they could see Martha's boy from Canada. It was like seeing my mother at different stages of her life, as the sisters all had the same features. This younger one looked like my mother had several years before. Another one was what my mother would look like in a few years. It was an odd sensation to meet them and feel that my mother was in that person.

One of the sisters lived in a nearby village called Holt. We went there for tea, and in the course of the conversation my aunt Rose asked, "Has it gone off yet?" My other aunt said no, but someone was coming to look at it in a couple of days. Once we were back on the bus I asked Aunt Rose what that was all about and quite casually she said, "Oh, a few nights ago one of the German planes bombing Bristol dropped a land mine in Holt and it is buried in the ground at the end of the yard." At this stage of the war such events were no longer novelties and the English people took them in stride with a minimum of fuss!

The youngest of my aunts had married late in life and her husband had been a widower and an ironmonger. He was a charming old gentleman and beat me quite handily in a game of chess. On one of my visits he called me to a window to see a bird. It sang and I said, "Oh. A coocoo."

He seemed quite upset and said, "Not a coocoo, a *cuckoo*!" He had me say it several times until I got it straight!

My cousin Beryl was a lovely person, in her mid-twenties. She worked at an airplane factory, to which she rode back and forth on her bicycle. She was able to get home for the noonday meal, which was usually the main meal of the day, with meat and vegetables and dessert washed down with cups of tea. Beryl would go to the movies with me, and I was always disappointed when her boyfriend Michael Smith visited. They were married after the war, and in later years I got to know him and he was the salt of the earth.

Beryl decided she would make me a real Canadian pie with a crust both on the top and on the bottom. It would be thin and not deep-dish as the English pies always were. The pie was duly made and baked and, when it was brought to the table, there in the centre was the ever-present egg cup used to hold up the top crust—which of course was a necessity in a deep dish pie. However, it was not needed in a thin pie and it sat there covered by dough and serving no purpose whatsoever! The pie was delicious and I made no comment about the odd look of it.

* * *

Once, while walking with my aunt, we passed a house and she told me that this particular house had had a lovely wooden picket fence but it had been knocked over and destroyed by a tank a couple of years before. Years later, I was talking to a co-worker and mentioned Trowbridge. He had been a tank driver during the war, and he said he knew the town. He told me he had been stationed just outside of Trowbridge, and while trying to negotiate a narrow road with his tank he had knocked down a picket fence!

While on leave I would go shopping with my aunt, which included a stop at the fishmonger's, as fish was a staple food in Britain. The usual varieties were long gone and most of the fish, if still whole, looked quite strange. My aunt would pick out one and ask if she should perhaps bake it. The shopkeeper would say "NO! NO! You better boil that one, mum, or it will be tough!"

My uncle was a delivery man for a furniture store and sometimes when he would make a delivery to a farmhouse they would give him something from the farm for a tip. Once when I was there it was a duck's egg and there was nothing for it but that Bob had to have the duck's egg. I enjoyed it and still buy them when I can find them.

On my first visit, my aunt asked what I would like to have to eat that was English. I said "crumpets," having never had them before, and that was the only food I could think of on the spur of the moment. She was surprised, but bought some, which we had for tea. Every time I have one now I think of that tea with the crumpets.

My aunt and uncle had two boys: Bob, who was the elder, and Cecil. Bob was off in the army somewhere and Cecil had been posted to the Middle East near the end of the war. He had a girlfriend, Dorothy Boyle, and she took me on buses to see old buildings, castles, and other beautiful homes, so that I saw more of the area than my mother had when she lived there. With my sense of balance I was the world's worst dancer, but I took Dorothy to one dance—or, more likely, Dorothy took me. All the other girls were with enlisted men and I was the only officer; later, Dorothy said all the other girls were jealous! The orchestra began to play a waltz and I told her I could not waltz. She said something like, "Rubbish. Of course you can," and led me onto the dance floor. I can still hear her shouting, "One, two, three" in my ear as I waltzed for the first and probably the last time.

One time I saw Aunt Rose's milkman. He came down their street with his wagon pulled by an old and tired-looking horse. On the wagon was a large wooden barrel containing milk he had brought from his farm. My aunt went out with a pitcher, which he filled up using a large ladle. It was obvious the milk had not been pasteurized, and how clean it was kept during its trip from the farm to the townspeople could only be guessed at. However, no one ever got ill drinking it, so it must have been all right.

I had one leave over Christmas and of course I went to Trowbridge. My aunt and uncle invited two soldiers from a nearby American camp, and they had dinner with us. They brought a large box with them containing all sorts of goodies including candy, cookies, cakes, and so on that the British had not been able to get for years. It was a wonderful Christmas celebration.

* * *

On one of my leaves I witnessed an event that has stuck in my mind ever since, especially when I put clothes into a modern-day washing machine. It was a Monday, the day used throughout Britain and her colonies by good British people everywhere, to do the laundry.

In the corner of the kitchen there was a bricked-in portion of the wall that formed a triangle, and behind the bricks was a large copper tub. The brickwork was open at the top and bottom.

First things first. On arising, my aunt put several pennies in the gas meter in order to obtain a good supply of hot water. Once heated, this water was transferred to the copper tub by means of a pail. Then in the bottom opening a coal fire was built to get the water boiling. A chimney ran from the fire, inside the wall, up to the roof, so there was no smoke inside the kitchen. Once steam was rising from the tub, in went the laundry to be boiled for quite some time.

When my aunt was satisfied that the clothes had boiled long enough, she got a piece of smooth wood about three feet long and fished them out into a tub, which was carried outside to the back yard. There sat a marvellous contraption, the like of which I had never seen before, nor since for that matter. Even Rube Goldberg would have been amazed!

It looked like two kettle drums joined in the middle. Each drum was lined by a metal container that could hold water, and in the middle of this wondrous gadget a wringer was fastened. It was about four or five feet long. The pail was again pressed into service to bring hot water from the kitchen, and this was poured into one side and then cold water was poured in the other side. Each kettle drum had wooden slats fastened together in the shape of a curve matching the bottom of the drum. This latticework was set about halfway down the depth of the water, and was connected to a handle that protruded from the side of the drum.

The laundry was dumped into the hot water and then the heavy work began. Grasping the handle, my aunt pushed and pulled it back and forth, and the wooden slats inside the tub steadily beat the clothes! When the laundry was considered to be clean, it was run through the wringer into the cold water. There it received another beating from the wooden slats on that side to get any soap out. Finally it was again run through the wringer and then hung up on the clothesline to dry.

The thought of Aunt Rose going through this procedure every Monday—if it was fine, of course—or out in the cold in the winter, boggled the mind. Still she seemed to think it was the most natural thing in the world that laundry should be done in this way. It was a hard life for a housewife indeed.

* * *

Our luck continued to hold, and Con and I were both posted to No.8 Advanced Flying Unit (AFU), which was located in the middle of the Isle of Anglesey in Wales, where we would have an orientation course to get us acquainted with flying and navigating in England.

Reg and Rose Cleverley with Beryl; my aunt, uncle and cousin with whom I spent most of my leaves.

Author

Beryl Jupp, my cousin who made the Canadian apple pie. When she married Michael after the war, she became Beryl Smith. She often said that the next time around she would call herself Mrs. Jupp–Smythe, which sounded much more sophisticated and upper class! Unfortunately, Beryl died in her late forties from a heart problem.

Author

CHAPTER 4

MONA

We arrived at the Advanced Flying Unit (AFU) on June 13th, 1944. It was situated more or less in the centre of the Isle of Anglesey near a small town called Henelgwys. The Isle of Anglesey was once known as "Mona," and was one of the last strongholds of the Druids when they were driven west. It was separated from the mainland by the Menai Strait, which was crossed at one spot by a bridge. Just two miles from the bridge on the island was Llanfair P.G. We drove by this little village's train station, which had an extraordinarily long platform to accommodate the sign bearing the town's name. It was Llanfairpwllgyngllgogerychyrrndrobwillanty-siliogogogoch! The name actually contains directions as to how to get to the village and means, "The church of St. Mary by the hollow of the white aspen, over the whirlpool, and St. Tysilio's church close to the red cave." Later, when our crew had been formed, our Welsh wireless operator tried to teach me how to say the name. I never made it past the first couple of syllables, and any Welshman would have cringed at my pronunciation.

We were Course 51, and started flying on June 15th. It was a night flight and I was second navigator. We flew eleven times with six day trips and five night exercises. The flights lasted anywhere from an hour and fifteen minutes to three hours and forty minutes. All were in twin-engine Ansons. At this point in our training, we were beginning to think that there was no other aircraft.

Some trips were over the sea and some were over land. A number of times we flew over South Stack, which was on Holy Island in the northwestern corner of the island. From the air it was a beautiful sight to see the small green island, the white lighthouse, and the adjacent buildings on the point with the blue sea all around.

Before starting our training we were told not to overshoot our station or we would find ourselves in Snowdonia, the high mountain range to the southeast. We were also warned in no uncertain terms that if we landed in Ireland and were interned we would be tried for desertion after the war. At best we would serve a long prison term; at worst we would be shot!

One day when we were not flying we were taken to a public bath. There we were given bathing suits, and after we had put these on, we were told to get into the pool. There was a large dinghy already in the pool, upside down. We were told we had to be able to turn the dinghy right side up and climb in, as we might well find ourselves in such circumstances at a later date. One at a time we had to accomplish this feat. We were wearing life preservers, which was a good thing, as I could not swim. When it was my turn I paddled over to the dinghy and after some strenuous pulling on the ropes affixed to the dinghy and pushing with my feet, I managed to turn it over. The problem was, I turned it over on top of myself! It seemed that I was under water for ages before I managed to get out from under and get my head above water. Mercifully the instructor did not make me try it again.

When the course was over we were given the names of three or four Operational Training Units (OTU) and we could sign up for the one to which we wished to be posted. This was the only time I ever remember this happening; usually you were just told where to go. Most of the fellows chose stations near London in order to enjoy the delights of that city. However, two navigators were needed in an OTU in northern Scotland and as we wanted to stay together, Con and I put our names down for that one. Again we were lucky, as that is where we were posted, arriving at No. 19 OTU on July 11th, 1944.

OPERATIONAL TRAINING UNIT

When Con and I arrived in Forres we were billeted in what had once been an estate house in the town. It even had an elevator! It was named Burghy House, but that soon got changed to "Buggery House" by one and all.

After a few days we left Burghy House behind and moved into Nissen huts about a mile down the road from the airfield. Nissen huts were long metal buildings with rounded roofs, a door at each end, and a couple of windows on each side. In the winter they were cold and damp and they were heated by two small coal-burning stoves, one at each end of the hut.

The airmen previously living in these quarters had discovered that the stoves gave off much more heat if you removed the bricks from inside. As a result, when the stove was going full blast it heated up to a nice cherry red! Of course, the heat caused the metal to slightly buckle so some of the stoves looked a bit lopsided! You were allowed only one coal scuttle of coal per week for each stove.

The coal was kept in a compound surrounded by a high fence topped with barbed wire and a locked gate to protect it from the enemy— us! When the coal began to run out, a few officers would wait until dark and then raid the compound. One or two would climb the fence and throw lumps of coal back over the fence where it was gathered and taken inside. When the scuttles were full again everyone got back into the huts as quickly as they could. I served on the coal gathering group a few times and fortunately we were never caught.

This station was the one where crews would be formed; and after we had been there for a day or two, the pilots, navigators and bomb-aimers were told to report to a large room. I think tea was available. The idea was that you would mill about and try to find someone compatible to start the nucleus of a crew. I did not enjoy this type of arrangement, and was standing off to one side when a pilot and a bomb-aimer approached me. It was Menno Bartsch and Ernie Pollit.

Min's first words were, "How would you like a shit-hot pilot?" I said something like that was fine with me, as they both looked presentable. We talked for a while and during the conversation I told them I had led the course when I got my wing. Ernie was in his mid-twenties; and only just recently I found out that Menno was younger than I was. The other day I told him had I known that at the time, I would not have treated him with such respect! We were then barely twenty years old!

Our other crewmembers were assigned to us, and they were all sergeants. John Prosser was the wireless operator, Colin Hynd the flight engineer, Stan Hare the mid-upper gunner, and Jim Wagstaff the tail gunner. Prosser was a Welshman and so became "Taffy," Colin was a Scot and the rest of us were Canadians. Hare was a very quiet fellow and kept to himself. As our training proceeded, Min and Ernie chummed around together, while Taffy and I hit it off. We could not get together in each other's messes, but over the months ahead we attended movies, went to dinners in town, and developed a warm friendship. I have tried to locate Prosser since the war, but the name John Prosser in Wales is like John Smith in New York!

The oldest member of our crew was Wagstaff. We all liked him and felt sorry when once he overslept and missed a training flight with us. He was waiting when we landed and of course Min had to chew him out and the poor fellow felt terrible.

Shortly after this episode someone thought it would be a good prank to toss a thunderflash into Wagstaff's hut. A thunderflash was like a firecracker that gave a loud bang when it exploded. They were used to simulate gunfire and explosions in training exercises.

Unfortunately, Wagstaff was struck in one eye by a piece of the thunderflash, and his flying days ended on the spot.

We were assigned a new tail gunner, a Yorkshireman named Southwell. He had a broad accent and to him all good things were "champion." When Min asked the crew if something was all right we would reply "OK," or something similar, but Southwell always said, "It's champion!"

Forres was the last OTU to use Whitley aircraft, as the other OTUs had all switched to Wellingtons. As a result the aircraft were old and many were unserviceable. On one occasion Min could not get up enough speed to get the plane off the ground, and we had to switch to another aircraft. On one flight the window beside Min was partly open. He gave it a rap to close it and the whole windscreen flew off! My log and chart whooshed off my desk and Min had to get us back down with a 100-knot wind blowing in his face.

One of Taffy's jobs kept him busy chewing great wads of gum. Pipes of glycol ran past his station and they kept springing leaks that he would plug up with gum! The Whitley flew in a nose-down position and the fuselage was a square shape, so it was called "The Flying Coffin." It also earned this name for another reason. There were twenty-nine crews, each with seven men, in our course and by the time the course ended nine aircraft had crashed, killing sixty-three airmen. The pilot of one of these crews had the bed next to mine. One morning before we had gotten up there was a terrible

The Wentworth Armstrong Whitley—a.k.a. "The Flying Coffin." One oddity of this aircraft was its length; the rear gunner had to crawl down a long tunnel that ran the length of the fuselage, and so wriggle into his turret.

British Columbia Aviation Museum

crash, and later in the day someone came and collected his belongings. That made you stop and think.

We worried about crashing to the point we went around the countryside surrounding the station looking for places on the hills or in banks of tall ferns and other likely spots where Min could hope for a safer landing if we did crash and he could get us to that point. Our closest call came one day when Min had to abort a landing at the last minute. In the Whitley the wheels had to be cranked up and down by hand and for the landing they were in the down position. I was in the copilot's seat and began to turn the crank as fast as I could to retract the landing gear. However we were heading directly towards two tall chimneys in Forres that were close together and the drag of the wheels kept us below their height. Just as we were about to hit them and shear off our wings, Min sideslipped between them, standing the plane practically on one wing. We emerged on the other side none the worse for wear except for rapidly beating hearts! At least mine was, as I had a front-seat view of the episode!

We practiced abandoning the aircraft. This was done on the ground. We all took our places and then Min would give the order to abandon the aircraft. Sometimes we were barely in our positions when the order came, and sometimes Min kept us waiting quite a while to try and catch us off guard. When we heard his order we acknowledged it, each in turn from the front of the plane to the rear. The bomb-aimer immediately opened a trap door in the floor near the nose and he and I dropped through it to the ground. The wireless operator, the engineer, and the mid-upper gunner jumped out of a door in the side of the plane. The rear gunner simply turned his turret around and tumbled out backwards. Once Min had heard everyone's acknowledgement, he went out through the door near the nose. Gradually we got better at the drill, and eventually were able to complete the operation in nineteen seconds from the time Min said, "Bail out!" until his feet were on the ground. When inspection time came we passed without a problem.

* * *

Our longest training flight, which lasted six hours and forty-five minutes, was laid out in the shape of a square taking us northwest from Forres over northern Scotland and the Atlantic. Most of the flight was to be over water; but as we were over clouds all the way and with hardly any navigational aids in the Whitley, I had to navigate by dead reckoning. This is simply projecting what course should be flown in future to stay on track when you have little or no information on which to base your calculations, other than the original data given to you on the ground before you set out.

We were far from the war zone so there was next to nothing for the bomb-aimer and the gunners to do, and only the pilot, the wireless operator, and I were busy. Come to think of it, the Whitley had no mid-upper turret so I am not sure what Hare did at any time on this course!

On the westward leg, Taffy was able to pick up a signal and with his directional finder he gave me a bearing on the station and I plotted it on my chart. About twenty minutes later, he got another bearing for me from the same radio station. Allowing for the distance we had travelled after getting the first signal, I was able to obtain a fix on our position and calculate a course for Min to fly to continue that leg of the trip. That was the only help I got!

Finally, on the leg home, Min asked when we would reach base. I told him we should be crossing Moray Firth near Forres in about a minute. Thirty seconds later there was a break in the clouds and there below us was Moray Firth and we were exactly where I had told him. I am sure my stock went up with the crew and I gained their confidence in my abilities as their navigator. I was pleased at the time, but eventually I came to believe that perhaps all the errors I had made when we were outward bound had been cancelled out by the errors I had made on the way back, all making for a "perfect" exercise in navigation!

* * *

On some flights Min and the gunners practised "corkscrews." If you were attacked by a fighter, one of the gunners would shout, "Corkscrew port [or starboard] GO!" Min would immediately turn the plane and dive and then turn the opposite way and climb. This resulted in the plane going through the sky on a corkscrew path and hopefully would not give the fighter such a good target. The Whitley answered such commands sluggishly, and it took brute strength to get the aircraft to respond. At times Min would haul back on the control column with his feet braced on the dashboard and it would seem forever until the craft came out of the dive.

* * *

If you were shot down over Germany or any other occupied country, and escaped immediate capture, you were to try to contact the underground and stay away from the enemy. To let you see what this might be like without any danger attached, our station had an exercise that was quite a bit of fun.

Our crew was placed in a van that had no windows; or if it had, they were blackened over so you could not see out. You were given a topographical map and driven around for an hour or more. The van twisted and turned so that you had no idea in which direction you were heading, and no idea of where you were when the van stopped. The doors at the back were opened and you piled out to find yourself on a lonely dirt road with high hedges on either side. The van drove off.

You had to find your way back to the station with just the topographical map to guide you. Because of the possibility of an invasion, all road signs had been removed, so you got no help there. To make the task more difficult, the Home Guard and the local police had been alerted, along with your own military police, to be on the lookout for you and if you were caught, back you went into the van and were driven even farther away. I would guess the initial drop-off was five to ten miles away from the station.

As Min was our captain, he commanded the crew as usual. We all studied the map and then set out in the direction we thought we should follow. There was no walking down roads, as from time to time a patrol drove by looking for crews; so we had to keep to the fields. When we came to a road we all huddled in the ditch while Min made sure the coast was clear, and then on his signal we tore across the road one by one and fell into the ditch on the other side.

Towns had to be avoided, as the local population knew what was going on and would join in the fun by reporting you to the local constabulary. At one point in our hike we came to an apple orchard and the apples were just right for a pick-me-up. One or two other crews had the same idea, and after a short rest we set off again. We had started out just after lunch and our map reading must have been pretty good, as we sighted the station just before suppertime. We were quite pleased that we had not been caught.

We were at the back of the station and had one more field to cross. About 100 yards from the buildings, a drainage ditch ran across the field. It was just a foot or two wide, and the water was only a few inches deep. As luck would have it, I slipped just as I went to step across and one foot went into the water up to my ankle. The remainder of my walk was step, squish, step, squish!

* * *

The air force tried to assist us as much as they could in the event we had to bail out over enemy territory. From time to time, an airman who had been shot down and managed to contact the underground and eventually get back to England, came and lectured on how he had done this and gave us tips on what we should do if we found ourselves in similar circumstances. They were interesting tales, and we listened to these fellows, as our lives might depend on what they were telling us.

One of the buttons on our battledress jacket came apart and one side of it was actually a very small compass. The button looked exactly like the other buttons on our uniform and didn't appear as though one could pull it apart, as the two halves snapped together securely.

One day our picture was taken wearing civilian clothing. We were given a shirt, a tie, and a suit jacket. The jacket and shirt were a size too large, to give the appearance we had lost weight. A picture somewhat like a passport photo was taken and you were told to look glum, as if you had been under Nazi rule for several years. This picture, about two inches square, was kept in a breast pocket and if we were successful in contacting the underground they would use the picture in forged travel or identification documents.

You also had a whistle attached to the collar of your jacket. If you had to ditch and were adrift in water, you could use it to attract any rescue party within earshot. Fortunately we never had to use any of these items.

None of us could speak a word of German, but some of the fellows who had managed to get back to England had been in the same boat. One of the airmen had bailed out near the front line and set out west toward the Allied armies. He contacted an American patrol who almost shot him, as they would not believe his story—he had just walked right through a minefield. Another fellow's plane had crashed head-on into the crest of a hill. The rest of his crew were killed, but he had been shot like a bullet out through the windscreen into a swamp. He hit the marsh in a flat trajectory and slid through the muck for yards before coming to a halt; at which point he picked himself up and walked away with only some cuts and bruises.

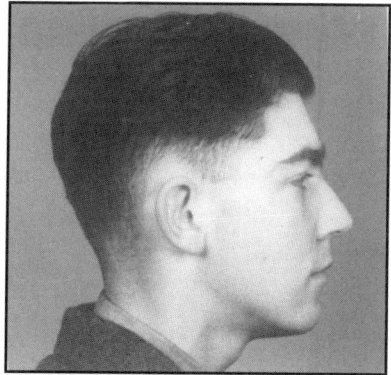

Passport photo, German version. A print of this photo was kept in the breast pocket of my battledress. In the event I had to bail out over Germany, the picture was to be given to the underground, if possible, to use it in manufacturing travel papers to aid my escape. I do look unhappy under Nazi rule!

Author

* * *

At OTU you had to make all your flights as a crew once it had been assembled. If you missed a flight you were dropped from that crew and assigned to another that was not as far advanced in the course.

Toward the end of our stay at Forres, I caught a cold. I should not have flown, but by now I was familiar with the crewmembers and had a great admiration for Min—so I flew.

The planes were of course not pressurized, so the higher you flew, the lower the air pressure. The air pressure in your sinus cavities was greater than the pressure outside and built up to the point where it would force open the diaphragm and air would escape. The reverse took place as you flew lower, and the greater outside pressure forced air in. Under normal conditions this posed no problem, but with a cold the air passages became blocked. The result was far different air pressures in the sinus cavity and the outside air.

As we flew higher it became apparent to me that my sinuses were completely blocked and the pain became excruciating. I continued to navigate with tears rolling down my face and only gained some relief when we descended to a lower altitude. I did not mention this to anyone, and I had a splitting headache for a day before my cold got better and everything became unblocked. For some years afterward I had sinus problems when I had a cold. It was a stupid thing to do, but fortunately I had no more colds while flying.

* * *

At one point in the winter the weather was so bad, and everyone was so damp, cold and miserable, the CO split the station in half and gave everyone a forty-eight-hour pass. When one-half were back on base, the other half left. No actual passes were issued and you were told in no uncertain terms you would be in deep trouble if you did not return when you were supposed to. Taffy and I went into Inverness and got a room in a hotel. What luxury it was to be warm, have a soft bed to sleep in, and to eat in the hotel's dining room!

* * *

I had met Madelyn at night school when I was sixteen years old, and for me it was the proverbial love at first sight. We began to see each other, going to movies, going for long walks, having picnics on the islands across from the Toronto harbour, and just sitting and talking. She was like an angel to me and it was over a year before I got up enough nerve to kiss her goodnight. By the time I was posted overseas I knew that Madelyn was to be my whole life.

During that time a fellow whom Madelyn had known since she was a child pursued her. He was going through for the ministry and was a conscientious objector. He was older than Madelyn, whereas I was younger; and he was much more sophisticated. He could say lovely things to her in Greek and write poetry for her. I found this out later but did not know it at the time. I only knew I didn't stand a chance—but I could hope.

During the winter of 1944/45 I received letter from Madelyn. She had come to realize that it was me whom she loved, and wrote to tell me I should not worry about other suitors. However, she did not spell it out plainly in the letter, and what she was trying to tell me was so vague that I had no idea what she was trying to say. So I continued to hope while she waited for my return.

* * *

At last, in January 1945, our stay at Forres ended and we were not unhappy to be rid of the Flying Coffins. At our next station, we would graduate to four-engine aircraft, the Halifax, which we would eventually fly in combat. We had spent almost eighty-three hours in the air in Whitleys and we were lucky to have escaped with our lives.

CONVERSION UNIT

On Jan. 5th, 1945 our crew was posted to 1658 Conversion Unit in Yorkshire, where Menno would learn to fly the four-engine Halifax bomber and the rest of the crew would become familiar with it as well. We were on the station a little over two months and during that time we flew twenty-two times. Seventeen of these trips were with Menno and for five flights we had other pilots. Seven flights were at night and fifteen were during the day. On a few trips we had an instructor on board to check us out, and he flew as a second pilot sitting beside Menno.

Most of the trips were either very short practice flights—one was for only twenty-five minutes—or bombing practice for Menno and Ernie, or slightly longer trips for navigation practice. Bombing practice was carried on just off the coast. There a wooden triangle had been built in the water and Ernie did bombing runs up to the target and dropped dummy bombs, trying to get them in the triangle.

Near the end of our course we were sent on two flights that for some strange reason were designated "sweepstakes"! These were both at night. On these flights a number of planes flew from our station toward the Danish coast. As you approached the coast the engineer dropped "window." This was the name given to strips of metal of a certain length which, when thrown from the aircraft in bundles, scattered and appeared as aircraft on the German radar screens. Anyone watching the screen would hopefully think a large bomber stream was approaching. The idea was that the Germans would divert fighters to intercept this non-existent stream from areas where the actual bombing was to take place.

At a given spot off the Danish coast we turned back to base. There was always some danger that fighters would fly out from the coast to actually attack, but we never encountered any on our two flights. That was not to say these flights were uneventful.

On one of these trips, when returning across the North Sea, we saw a light flashing on the water below. There seemed to be no rhyme or reason to the flashes, as none of our crew who saw the light could decipher any Morse code message and the flashes did not spell out an SOS. It may have been a small boat trying to escape German-occupied Denmark. If it had been someone in a dinghy from a downed aircraft we thought they would have known some Morse code. In any event, we reported what we had seen when we attended the debriefing after the trip, but heard no more about it. Min said afterward that if it was a dinghy in the middle of the North Sea it was in an awful body of water! We had been told that the North Sea was very cold. Although salt water, it was only a couple of degrees above freezing. If you were immersed in it you were given only three or four minutes before you died from exposure.

On the other "sweepstake," we had an instructor along who was checking us out on our work, particularly Min on his flying of the Halifax. At the pre-briefing, the navigators had been given estimated wind speeds at the height we would be flying of thirty-five knots, with the wind coming from the north. For the first course I used this data to give Min the course to fly. Being near England, we were still able to obtain fixes from GEE without interference, so these would be quite accurate.

GEE was the code name given to a navigational aid. Radio signals were emitted by stations in England that were picked up in the aircraft on a screen, the reading of which signals translated into positions on the map.

The first fix I obtained showed us to be well south of track, and when I calculated the wind velocity I was amazed to get 200 knots! I thought surely I had made some mistake, but my calculations after the next fix showed a wind velocity of 250 knots—even worse—and we were farther south of track than ever! I could not believe these figures, but I was sure my work was correct, so I hedged a bit and gave Min a course to bring us back on track using a wind speed of 150 knots.

As the wind was directly off our port side, the course in which this wind speed resulted had the aircraft pointing in a northeasterly direction, although if correct, the wind would be blowing us along the track we wanted. Min had a hard time believing this also and thought perhaps his compass was not working properly. Accordingly he asked the instructor to fly the plane while he went up into the astrodome and took a sighting with the astrocompass. This checked out, so I guess reluctantly he used the compass heading I had given him.

The strong winds lasted for most of the trip until we were nearly back at base and had reduced height to a lower level. We crossed the coast about ten miles south of our landfall. Had I used the wind speeds I had calculated, we would have returned to England on our proper track! We later learned that navigators who did not trust their findings and used the wind speeds given by the Met Office brought their planes in all along the coast, even down to the Thames estuary, where one plane was fired on by British anti-aircraft batteries, but fortunately escaped unharmed.

In later years meteorology discovered the jet stream. I doubt our met man on the station had ever heard of it, but it now seems obvious that that is what we had encountered.

Apart from flying, we had to attend many lectures, which to us seemed very boring. Quite often these talks were attended by a wing commander who, because of his rank, was allowed to bring his dog, a hideous-looking beast, all white with a black ring around one eye. He always had a few questions at the end of the lecture that prolonged matters, while the rest of us wanted to get back to the mess to relax. After a minute or two some of the fellows, who obviously made sure they were out of sight, began shouting at him to keep quiet, using terms that would not be acceptable in polite society.

Eventually we would finally be dismissed, but by this time, back in the mess others would have picked up the popular newspapers and we would be lucky if a copy of the *Times* was left on the coffee table. Everyone tried to get the *News of the World* to read. It was a scandal sheet, and along with the news of the war, it told all the juicy stories of who was doing what to whom in the ranks of the British upper crust.

Finally we completed our training and were posted to 158 Squadron, located at Lisset, Yorkshire. Here Con Eidt and I parted company, as his crew was sent to a different squadron. We had become closer to our own crews so we did not feel a great sense of loss, but simply wished each other good luck. To show that it is a small world indeed, Con Eidt survived the war, returned to Canada, and married one of my cousins! My cousin's family was a branch we seldom saw and I only learned of Con's marriage many years later.

We were excited that our training days were finally over and that we were going to start actually getting involved in operational flights and dropping bombs on the foe. Mixed with the excitement there was some apprehension of the unknown. In spite of all the training we had had, and while we were well disciplined in taking orders from Min and any other superior officer, we were still really young boys who had no idea of what fighting the war was all about and what we would find it to be like.

It was somewhere around this time that Min received a promotion to flight lieutenant and I was promoted to flying officer. This meant a little more pay, but not too much else except to our pride in the new insignia: Min received epaulets and two rings on his sleeve, and I now had a wider white ring.

CHAPTER 5

158 SQUADRON

The 158 Squadron, to which we had been posted on Mar. 5th, 1945, was located in Yorkshire east of Driffield and just a mile from the coastal village of Barmston. Seven miles farther along the coast was Bridlington, a seaside resort. This squadron had been formed in 1918, just a short time before the end of World War I. After being located at various aerodromes it was finally set up at Lisset in February 1943.

Our crew on joining 158 Squadron. Back row, left to right: John "Taffy" Prosser, the Welsh wireless operator; Southwell, the Yorkshire rear gunner who shortly thereafter had a nervous breakdown; Stan Hare, mid-upper gunner; Colin Hynd, the irreverent Scot, engineer, and our youngest member at nineteen. Front row, left to right: Ernie "Spike" Pollitt, Canadian, bomb-aimer, the old man at twenty-six; Menno "Min" Bartsch, Canadian, pilot and skipper of the crew; the author, Canadian landed immigrant, navigator.

Author

On arrival we walked along a path to one of the administration buildings to get our directions and orders. It was a dull day with solid cloud cover. The ceiling was very low, about 400 or 500 feet, and it almost seemed as though you could reach up and touch it. We heard the steady hum of an approaching aircraft, which turned into a deepening roar as the plane drew closer. Hidden in the cloud, it passed overhead and the hum began to fade in the distance.

Suddenly, as though in slow motion, a pair of feet appeared under the cloud, followed by legs, a body, and finally a parachute. Two further such figures appeared and slowly disappeared from our sight as they drifted behind some buildings and trees about half a mile away.

Such was our welcome to squadron. We did not find out what had happened, but could only guess they had bailed out after reaching base in a beat-up aircraft. There were many happenings on squadron that we were to learn were not discussed. Each crew lived in their own little world in the midst of the larger family.

While we had some apprehension as to what might lie ahead, we were in good spirits and expected everyone else to be the same. But over the next day or two, we found the other airmen to be quiet and moody. Finally we learned the reason for this. A day or two before we arrived, some of the squadron's aircraft had participated in a night raid. They were followed home by fighters who infiltrated the bomber stream. The fighters waited until the bombers were in the circuit or actually coming in to land; and when they were at their most vulnerable, the fighters attacked and shot down two of them, killing some of the crews. What made the event even more heartrending was the fact that the raid on Germany was over, and the crews would be feeling much relief at being back home safe and sound; they would have been relaxed and in good spirits when disaster struck.

A day or two after our arrival, we were told to present ourselves at 1600 hours the next day at the CO's home, as he wished to personally welcome all new crews. The CO lived in a small cottage at one side of the aerodrome. A little yard was surrounded by a white picket fence, and a gate opened onto a path leading to the front door. We arrived at the appointed time as polished as we could be and opened the gate. To my horror, there sat a large dog, all white with a large black circle around one eye! There could be no doubt. Our new CO was the Winco we had shouted at when we were at Conversion Unit!

If the CO recognized anyone he said nothing, and indeed we spent a pleasant hour having tea. However, I breathed a sigh of relief when the interview was over and we were back on our own turf.

* * *

For the commissioned ranks, the officers' mess was a wonderful spot. It was the hub of social activity, a place to meet with friends, a place to relax, a place for a drink, and a place to play simple games when you were not on duty.

The dining room was off to one side and you went through a wide doorway from it into the mess, and just before stepping inside you came smartly to attention. There were quite a number of easy chairs and sofas, end tables and coffee tables, a bar at one end, and a piano. I could play the piano a little by ear and once in a while I was pressed into service for singsongs. The tunes were always the same: "I've Got Sixpence," "White Cliffs of Dover," "Roll Me Over," "We'll Meet Again," and so on—all the favourites of the war years. We heard them over and over on the radio and I think their familiarity provided comfort.

Every day newspapers were put on a coffee table and were avidly sought after. The first to disappear was the *News of the World*, which contained all the bits of scandal; and if you were late getting to the table, there was the *Times* with the ads on the front page! A very dry read inside, although factual.

The two games were of course darts—which required some dexterity when the mess was full to avoid anyone getting hurt—and "Shove 'Apenny," which requires some explanation, as I have seen the game only once since then, and that was a showpiece rather than the actual game.

Sitting on one end of the bar was a board about thirty or forty inches long. At the far end there were lines drawn across the board. An 'apenny was placed on the end of the board nearest to yourself and it was positioned so that a bit of it protruded over the board's edge. You struck the coin with the heel of your hand so that it slid up the board. The object was to have it come to rest between the lines. Your opponent then did the same, with the object of knocking your coin off the board or getting between lines farther up the board. It was sort of a miniature type of shuffleboard.

The officers' dining room was cafeteria style. You lined up at one end, took a tray and proceeded along the aisle to pick up your meal. The food was good, and far better than the menu of the civilian population. There were roasts and chops with potatoes and other vegetables. The most common vegetable was simply called "greens," and was probably the leaves of beets or Swiss chard. You got used to it, although one fellow remarked he didn't mind being fed the leaves of trees but when they started putting in the branches too he was not amused! Off to one side there was a table with several types of cheese on it with crackers to finish off the meal. There was tea or coffee to drink.

Once as a special treat for the English airmen they served "jugged hare." Rabbits were hung for a lengthy period until they became "high," and were then cooked and served as a kind of stew with large chunks of the rabbit intact. Some one remarked that theirs was still moving, and that was enough. I think only the English fellows ate it.

Quite often when we lined up someone would be standing at the end of the line with a basket of lemons, and you were handed one as you passed by. They were supposed to help with your night vision. Min would peel his and break it into segments, eating it like an orange. He can still eat a lemon that way, much to the distress of anyone present.

I saved mine. My night vision was good and in any event I was always at work over my logs and charts, not peering into the darkness for fighters. I took them to my aunt's, and the first time I handed them over the family couldn't have been more pleased, as they had not even seen a lemon for years. They peeled one and each received a segment, which they ate, all the while grimacing and saying how sour it was, but enjoying it all the same.

Occasionally an American plane would have engine trouble and have to land at our base. The officers in their crew naturally ate in our mess. However, you had to wear jackets, and the only jacket they would have with them would be the bomber jacket they wore while flying. On the station were a number of career RAF officers who were somewhat stuffy and were prim and proper at all times. When one of the RAF types was behind an American wearing his bomber jacket, it was amusing to see the RAF officer looking everywhere but at the back in front of him emblazoned with a grinning Donald Duck or Mickey Mouse!

* * *

SOME NAVIGATIONAL AIDS

As the war progressed, improvements were constantly being made in the aircraft of Bomber Command. Newer types flew faster, higher, and farther than their predecessors—all of which complicated successful navigation to targets.

In the early years of flight, planes flew quite low and you could navigate by picking your way from place to place by map reading, or better still by following railway tracks from town to town. Once airplanes flew higher, you were often above clouds and could no longer see the ground and map read, but "dead reckoning" was relatively easy. If you knew the direction in which you wished to fly and your air speed—if it was not too fast—you could easily calculate your estimated time of arrival and course in order to offset the effect of the wind, which blew the aircraft off the required track. The faster you flew, the more difficult this became.

Scientists were continually looking for ways in which you could accurately fix your position and one of the first methods introduced in August 1941 was TR 1335, which became known as "GEE."

Three stations about 100 miles apart, located in England and later in France, produced pulse transmissions. One station transmitted a radio pulse and this simultaneously triggered pulses from the other two stations. These radio pulses radiated from the stations similar to the ripples on a pond when a stone is thrown into it. The aircraft was equipped with a receiver that measured the difference in time between receipt of the signals, and this was displayed on a cathode ray tube used by the navigator. The display consisted of blips above and below a central line running across the screen. One blip that remained constant was the aircraft, and the other blip represented the signal continuously moving across the screen as the aircraft's position kept changing in relation to the radar stations. Once the blips were aligned, a reading was taken and plotted on a special grid map and then transferred to the navigator's plotting chart.

The aircraft already had a gadget that was hooked up to the compass and airspeed indicator, and this showed you the latitude and longitude of the aircraft as though there were no wind at all. By comparing this position to the GEE fix you could see how far the wind had blown you off course, in what direction, and how far in a given period of time. Thus you knew the direction in which the wind was blowing and its speed. With this information it was easy using your slide rule to calculate a course to offset the wind and get you to where you wanted to go.

By January 1943, all of the aircraft of Bomber Command were equipped with GEE. Needless to say the Germans were not idle and soon found out how to jam the readings by producing radio pulses that were picked up by the aircraft and resulted in multiple blips on the screen. These could not be told from the real blip. The closer you came to the German stations, the more blips there were and finally you inevitably gave up trying to sort them out and GEE became useless until you were on the way home and again out of range of the interference.

For some reason or other when examining your logs the navigation officer always seemed to think you could have stretched the use of GEE, and seldom failed to comment on it. If only he could have seen the multitude of overlapping blips running amok across the screen! Of course he had on his own trips, but nevertheless this comment always raised my dander.

* * *

Another navigational aid, code-named "Oboe," was introduced in January 1943. It consisted of two ground stations transmitting radio pulses. These were arranged so that an aircraft flew along the arc of one pulse that was set up to cross over the target. The second pulse was transmitted to intersect, at more or less right angles, the first pulse over the target. When the second pulse was picked up by the aircraft, the bombs were dropped.

Oboe was accurate within 300 yards. The Germans did not completely succeed in jamming Oboe, but it had some limitations. At first only one plane at a time could use the system. This failing was corrected in due course. The higher one flew the greater the range, but few bombers reached 28,000 feet, where a maximum range of 270 miles was possible. Also, a bomber using Oboe had to fly a straight course along the arc, making it more vulnerable to fighter attacks. Accordingly, Oboe was used largely on Mosquito aircraft that flew higher and faster than the heavier, four-engine bombers. It was largely used by the Pathfinder Force to lay down markers.

For some strange reason the signal along which the aircraft flew was called the "cat" and the intersecting signal was called the "mouse."

Eventually the Germans developed their own version of Oboe and used it for raids on major cities where accuracy was not that important. The English scientists devised a method of bending the German's "mouse" signal and one night when the Germans were set up to bomb Bristol, they bent the signal so that it intersected the "cat" signal over Dublin! This neutral city was bombed, causing no end of consternation in diplomatic circles and the Germans seldom used it thereafter. One added cause for celebration by the Allies was that the German aircraft that bombed Dublin did not have enough fuel to get back to their base on the continent!

* * *

A navigational aid called "H2S" came into use toward the end of the war and was quite different from other inventions. It gave you a picture of the ground features over which you were flying. Radar equipment was placed under the plane that gave out pulses directed toward the ground. If these pulses met with a flat surface such as water, they bounced off at an angle away from the aircraft. If they met with irregular surfaces such as land, some of the pulses would be redirected back to the airplane and show up as a dim light on a screen. If the pulses encountered a built-up area with slanting roofs, most of the pulses would bounce straight back to the aircraft and show as a bright spot on the screen. Accordingly, shorelines would show up as black on the water side and lighter on the land side. Rivers would show as a black streak running through a lighter countryside, and cities would be very bright on the screen. The images were exactly the shape of the contours on the ground, so on the screen you would see every turn of a river or the exact shape of a city.

By the end of the war most bombers were equipped with H2S. A camera was mounted to one side of the screen and when you were over the target the navigator swung the camera around, pointing it at the screen, and snapped a picture, so that the brass knew for sure you were over the target and not dropping bombs in the wrong spot. On our last raid on Heligoland, we had to make two runs to get over the small target due to the number of planes trying to fly over the island at the same time; and when we were circling I took a picture of the H2S screen that showed Heligoland quite plainly.

* * *

"Fishpond" was a means of helping bombers be aware of approaching fighter aircraft. The device sent out radar pulses that were reflected back by any object near the plane. The returning signals were displayed on a cathode ray tube showing up as bright spots on the screen. As you were in a stream of bombers, all going the same direction and at the same speed, the other bombers near by showed up as white spots on the screen that did not move much in relation to the others. If a spot of light suddenly began to drift across the screen or change position radically, there was a good chance it was a fighter plane trying to infiltrate the stream.

The screen was monitored by the wireless operator, who advised the pilot and gunners if he saw something suspicious. He was able to tell them from which direction the trespasser was approaching, and whether or not it was coming in slowly or quickly. If nothing else, this gave you a certain sense of comfort on a dark, moonless night when the gunners could only spot other aircraft when they were very close indeed.

On one of our night flights I had a spare moment near the target and had a look at the screen just as a blip shot across from one side to the other. None of the crew spotted a plane, but I was impressed with the gadget's ability to show such action.

Once we started flying in the Halifax bomber, which was equipped with these aids, it was a navigator's dream. Before we only had visual sightings and the odd radio beam to help; but GEE and H2S made our job a lot easier.

* * *

TRAINING FLIGHTS

When it became time for us to begin operational flights, a fact that had to be considered was what would happen if Min were injured and could no longer fly the plane. Accordingly, it would be a good idea if one or two other members of the crew knew what to do in such an emergency. To this end once our crew was formed, from time to time when an opportunity presented itself, Ernie or I sat in the pilot's seat and Min gave us some instruction in flying the aircraft. Nothing elaborate, just the bare essentials to keep the plane flying straight and level, and how to make gentle turns.

On days when the sky had numerous cumulus clouds and one of us was sitting at the controls, Min would direct us to fly directly into a cloud. Then he would tell us not to pay attention to the instrument panel but to fly the plane as our instincts told us. Invariably when we came out the other side of the cloud a minute later we would be making a turn to the right or left and either be in a climb or descending. That soon taught us that we could not trust what our body was telling us—we must trust the instruments.

In southern England there were two or three airfields with extra-long runways. We were not expected to be able to land the plane properly, but we would go to such a field, get ourselves lined up with a runway and then fly the plane "into the ground." By that I mean, we kept getting lower until we were just a few feet above the ground, and then cut all switches and let the plane hit and slide down the runway. The wheels would of course be up, as we lacked the experience to make a proper landing; trying it with the wheels down could have resulted in terrible crashes, cartwheels, and numerous other events best left unsaid.

Fortunately we never had to try this exercise, as Min was never hurt and was always there, flying our plane safely home. Our training had taught us to trust all of our crewmates, but our trust in Min's flying ability was always paramount.

A phenomenon of nature came to our attention when we were on short training flights with not too much work to do. We would occasionally see a rainbow if we were in the right spot between the sun and a cloud or falling rain. When you see a rainbow on the ground it is in the form of an arc, because the horizon cuts off the lower part. In the air, if you are high enough, the rainbow forms a perfect circle! I was quite amazed the first time I saw this, as I had never thought that it would always be round, but that it would be kept to an arc as when viewed from the ground.

* * *

Soon after I arrived in England, Madelyn sent me a gift. It was a little leprechaun made out of pipe cleaners. They had been twisted to make arms and legs on a two-inch body. The whole was covered with a dark green felt including a little cap. In the letter enclosing the figure, she had inadvertently misspelled my name, leaving off the last "b." After that we called the leprechaun "Bo."

He was my good luck charm, and I carried him everywhere with me tucked into the breast pocket of my battledress. He had already accompanied me on a couple of ops, but one day when I got to the field I discovered I had left him behind when I had changed jackets. I jumped on my bicycle and tore back to the billet, found Bo and put him in his usual spot, then rode as quickly as I could back to the airfield. I arrived just in time to get suited up and board the plane for our flight.

Just recently I discovered that Min had always carried a little cloth rabbit in one of his pockets, which we did not know about. No doubt the other members of the crew carried their own secret good luck charms.

Unfortunately I don't know where Bo is now. I have moved many times since the war, mountains of trivia have been discarded, and he may have been thrown away, inadvertently, in one of the moves.

However, somehow I doubt that. I am now seventy-eight and I am having, still, a wonderful life. Somewhere in an envelope or a pocket in the dark recesses of a cupboard I think Bo is still watching over me!

* * *

I spent most of my leaves in Trowbridge with my aunt and uncle. Of course they had their own stories to tell of their experiences of the war, some of them quite interesting.

One evening when my Uncle Reg was on firewatch in his neighbourhood, he was walking beside the wall bordering the church property. He was a short man, perhaps only five foot six, and the eight-foot wall towered over him. Out of nowhere a German plane that had bombed Bristol flew over on its way back to Germany and, as it was flying very low, the crew decided to strafe Trowbridge. They seemed to be shooting straight at my uncle, and he saw the tracers flashing toward him. Without a thought he went up over the wall to get it between himself and the danger. After, when he related what had happened, he had no idea how he managed to get over such a high wall with his short stature!

There were always two or three bicycles standing in the lane beside my aunt's house, and one day when Beryl was off work, she, Dorothy and I went for a ride in the country outside of Trowbridge. Beryl knew of a spot where wild flowers grew, and we cycled there. A tiny corner in a field by the road was absolutely filled with wild flowers and we picked armfuls of them, putting them in the baskets at the front of the bikes. When we reached home, Aunt Rose put them in vases and there were flowers all over the living room.

One of the old buildings that Dorothy took me to see had at one time been a small castle with a moat around it. The moat was now dry and the drawbridge had disappeared, but there were still the remains of an old gate. Just inside the gate was a small building that had been the church, and on one wall was a painting that must have been done perhaps a thousand years before. It was of a religious theme and although it was faded, you could make out the figures quite well.

On one of my visits to Dorothy's home I had a cold. Her mother and father thought I should take something for it and Mr. Boyle poured me a small tot of Scotch to have after supper. I sipped this while sitting in front of a warm fireplace and, not being used to liquor, I fell fast asleep. Mrs. Boyle had to shake me awake much later in the evening so that I would not miss my bus back into Trowbridge.

There was always something of interest to see on my train rides to Trowbridge. On one such trip I had to change trains at Bristol. I had only a few minutes, and walked down to the end of the platform and looked around the end of the wall. The station was in downtown Bristol and what greeted my eyes was a vast wasteland of rubble stretching for blocks and blocks. There was not a building standing in this area. The whole centre of the city had been destroyed by German bombing! I never saw anything like it again, but it gave me a vivid idea of what the German cities must look like that we were devastating with our raids. It was odd that while downtown Bristol had been wrecked, it was the suburbs of Bath, a city not that many miles away, that had been hard-hit by the bombing.

The train from Bristol to Trowbridge often picked up schoolchildren, mostly in their teens, and when that happened you were in for a noisy ride. However, I did not mind, as it was marvellous to hear the young voices and their laughter in the midst of the trying times Britain was having.

One train I took on my way back to camp, from Hull up to Bridlington, was an early morning milk run. The train would barely reach ten miles per hour, when it would stop and there would be a great deal of clanking while more milk cans were loaded on board. It took three or four hours to make the fifty-odd miles!

CHAPTER 6

ESSEN

We knew it was bound to happen sooner or later, but still it was a bit of a shock to be awakened at 0730 on March 11th, 1945, and told that our crew would be taking part in an operational bombing mission that day. Twenty-three aircraft from our squadron were to take part, and we were one of those crews. At last our training was at an end and we were faced with the real thing.

We had breakfast at eight and were told that the main briefing would be held at 0930. It was an odd feeling and one that was probably shared by the rest of the crew. I was not really afraid, but there was a feeling of apprehension about the unknown. The war movies we had seen had shown German fighters screaming across the bomber stream with cannons firing and tracer bullets whizzing by. In the excitement, sometimes there was panic in the voices of the crew as the gunners fired their machine guns. Would it be like that? The slogan "Even the walls have ears" extended into the life of the squadron, and talk in the mess usually consisted of light banter with no—or very little—mention of operational flights. We therefore had no first-hand accounts from experienced crews to allay—or perhaps add to—our fears.

Occasionally we would hear what was considered a funny story by some, but was probably quite frightening to those involved. One navigator was on his last flight to complete a tour when a piece of shrapnel from an anti-aircraft shell burst through the side of the plane. It went over his shoulder and splintered on his table. His chart was torn to shreds but he did not receive a scratch. Some thought his efforts to continue navigating using a chart made up of shreds of paper were hilarious!

Just after nine o'clock, crews began to drift into the hall for the main briefing. No one told us what the drill was so we just followed everyone else like sheep. The hall was used for a movie theatre and was filled with row upon row of straight-backed chairs. The room became steadily noisier as more crews crowded in. Then at 0930 a voice at the front shouted, "ATTEN-*SHUN!*" There was a scraping of chairs as all got to their feet; and then absolute silence.

Wing Commander Read, who in his own flying days had been an air gunner, threw back the covering that had been hiding a map set up on an easel, and with a long pointer indicated that the target was Essen in the Ruhr. The Allied armies were poised on the Rhine about fifteen miles away, ready to fight their way into the heart of Germany; it had been decided to strike a devastating blow to the munitions plants still operating in the Ruhr valley, despite many previous bombing attacks, especially the Krupp works in Essen. As well, the major cities of the Ruhr were used as points through which German troops were conveyed to the front and would also be used as escape routes when the Allies crossed the Rhine. A massive raid would block roads and create chaos. Accordingly, Bomber Command had laid on over 1,000 aircraft for this one operation.

The CO then turned the briefing over to other senior officers, who spoke briefly about their own trades. A meteorologist gave a report on the kind of weather that could be expected, the direction and force of the expected winds, cloud cover, and so on. It was a Sunday and one hard-hearted and battle-weary officer said to the assembly, "We should catch all the little Nazi bastards coming out of Sunday school." There was a small ripple of laughter but I think most were as uncomfortable with this remark as I was. In a bomber you were high above the earth, removed from the horrors of the ground; and it was disquieting to have what you were in fact doing brought to your attention.

On a lighter note, we were told to take a shower before takeoff. We didn't question this, but just followed orders. Hindsight suggests this was not based on your mother's advice to wear clean underwear in case you were in an accident, but so that you would be clean and any wounds suffered would be less likely to get infected.

After again rising and standing at attention for the CO's departure, the main briefing ended. Immediately the room was again filled with the babble of voices, only now the air was filled with excitement. The various trades then went their separate ways to their own sections for briefings. I followed along with the other navigators and we soon found ourselves provided with logs and charts and sitting at tables copying down information on the top of our log from a blackboard at the front of the room. The information we were given set out the track we were to follow to the target, expected wind speeds and directions on each leg, courses to be flown if the wind data was correct, and so on. These pieces of info made a good base from which to start, but once in the air we would calculate our own winds and navigate accordingly.

Around eleven a.m. we were given a meal. Eggs were in very short supply in England so as a special treat we were given bacon and eggs. It is difficult to prepare a meal for a lot of people and keep it hot, and without today's modern equipment it is impossible. As a consequence the bacon and eggs were barely warm and hence very greasy. We could have enjoyed a much better lunch in the officers' mess but once we knew the target, we were segregated from the other crews and the mess was off-limits. Dessert was bread and jam, the jam being another treat, due to sugar rationing. In any event we were young and our stomachs were able to cope.

After the meal we donned our flying gear and were taken by truck to the aircraft we were to use. It turned out to be "X-Xray," and we used this plane for all but one of our flights. We piled out of the truck, awkward in our flying boots and flying suits with our parachute harnesses strapped on. We were carrying our parachutes, and I also had a large canvas bag containing my navigational equipment. I once saw a cartoon of a navigator struggling under his load; the caption said: "Carry on Canada!"

Before we clambered into the aircraft, Min perhaps for luck walked under the bomb bays, which were still open, and inspected the bomb load consisting of fifteen 500-pound bombs. Min walked up to the bomb in the centre of the bay, licked the fingers of his right hand, and slapped the bomb. He carried out this ritual on all subsequent ops, and we always waited until he had performed this action before getting on board.

* * *

Once on board the aircraft we took up our stations. Min of course sat in the pilot's seat in the cockpit on the left-hand side. To his right, the bomb-aimer sat throughout the flight until he moved up to the nose for the bombing run and picture taking. I sat between those two and the nose, facing the left side of the aircraft and with my head about level with Min's feet. Behind the cockpit, the wireless operator sat at a small desk on which rested his key. The engineer was to the rear of the wireless operator with a jump seat to sit on. In the middle of the aircraft the mid-upper gunner sat on a swivel chair with his head in a Plexiglas dome where he could scan the sky to either side and above the plane. Finally the rear gunner sat in his turret facing to the rear.

We were scheduled to take off at 1140 and start our first leg at 1210 from base to the first turning point. After all checks of our equipment had been performed, Min started up the engines and they gradually developed into a roar. He gave the signal for "chocks away" and, after receiving notice from the control tower, we joined the other planes lining up for takeoff. The runway that was usually used was directly in line with a farmhouse, and one after another the aircraft went straight over the building at about 100 feet up. The roar must have been deafening. I wondered what the people thought, if in fact anyone was living there during the war.

We took off at 1205. Our first leg was to be flown at 8,000 feet, so during the climb to this height we circled the station. Twenty-two other aircraft were doing the same thing and a sharp lookout had to be kept to avoid midair collisions. The aircraft from 158 Squadron having reached 8,000 feet all closed on the station strung out across part of the sky and it was not possible for all to fly exactly over the station as they were supposed to do. Finding a slot in the gaggle of aircraft we crossed base and started on our first leg at 12:13, three minutes late.

Our first two legs were more or less a straight line down to Reading, where we were to turn and head out over the English Channel a few miles west of Brighton. I used the wind speeds and directions given at the briefing to give courses to Min during the first few minutes of the flight, and then began to calculate my own. To begin with I had given Min a course of 187 and an airspeed of 205 knots and I found this was taking us slightly right of track—only a couple of miles, but the object was to navigate so that you ran along the track as though you were on rails. I gave Min a course of 181 at an air speed of 205 and that brought us to the edge of Reading. As we proceeded, more and more aircraft joined the stream, forming a vast armada of planes strung out over a wide area of England. On training flights we had had the skies more or less to ourselves—or so it seemed—but now the number of kites around us was staggering.

At the time I never gave it a thought, but in later years I wondered how the inhabitants of Reading survived the constant noise of aircraft day after day as all of the bomber streams made their turn toward the continent at that point. The noise of the aircraft must have been almost continuous except when the weather was bad. At the same time, you had to wonder if the people in Reading didn't get some comfort from the sound of their own aircraft heading toward the continent, striking a blow for them that they themselves could not.

The next leg took us from Reading to the middle of the English Channel, and from there we had a long, straight line into southern

Belgium. We were bang on track all the way through this section; and halfway along this stretch we began to climb to reach 20,000 feet, the height from which we were to bomb. Once over the channel, on Min's instructions, each gunner fired his weapon for a short burst in order to make certain it was operating properly. We were in bright sunshine, but below us the cloud cover was solid and the ground could not be seen. All around us were planes in a great convoy and it would have been possible just to sit back and follow the bomber stream in. As we got closer to Germany, the interference on the GEE box was very bad and I got my last fix at 1438, which showed us to be a couple of miles to the north of track.

We continued on, amazed at the number of bombers filling the sky. The bomb-aimer took his position in the nose and at 1500 hours the engineer commenced to drop window. As we approached Essen and the bomb-aimer took over, I had a few moments to look out. Somewhat lower than the level at which we were flying and off to our right and slightly ahead were perhaps a dozen puffs of smoke showing where anti-aircraft shells had burst. We were far enough away that we did not even feel any of the shock waves, let alone sustain any damage.

Great clouds of smoke were roiling up through the clouds from fires in the city below, which we could not see. All the time through our headsets we could hear two voices: the bomb-aimer giving directions to Min—"Left . . . left . . . steady . . . right . . . steady . . ."— and the master bomber, who was directing the raid from his own aircraft, telling the bomb-aimers at which coloured flairs to aim. These flares had been dropped by a pathfinder squadron, who were always the first over the target. They were the best crews and most of them had already completed one or two tours of duty. They dropped flares to mark the target to provide aiming points when cloud covered the ground or at night when visibility was not that great.

The master bomber flew well below the main bomber stream over the target area, which meant he had to contend with bombs dropping from above as well as anti-aircraft fire from below. He had to be low enough to see the ground to make sure the pathfinders had marked the proper spot. Usually the master bomber flew a Mosquito bomber, a twin-engine, very fast airplane with a two-man crew. Rolls Royce engines with 1,250 hp gave the Mosquito a top speed of 415 mph and a service ceiling of 40,000 feet, well beyond our capabilities of perhaps 250 mph and 25,000 feet.

On one of our ops we heard the master bomber suddenly say, "We have been hit. We have been hit. Take over green leader. We are going in. We are going in!" All of this was said in quite a calm voice, and then there was silence. I could not imagine anyone being so calm in such a situation; that person must have had nerves of steel.

We were to drop our bombs at 1511 and at precisely that moment the bomb-aimer gave the call, "Bombs gone." I noted this in my log with some satisfaction! It was then necessary for the pilot to fly straight and level for about thirty seconds while the bomb-aimer took pictures of the bomb bursts. In this case with all of the cloud cover the best the pictures would show was that he had bombed the correct coloured markers. The engineer who had been chucking window out of the side door for some minutes stopped doing this at 1521 hours.

We learned later that we had had fighter cover, but on this occasion the German fighters were non-existent and not a one was seen by any of the bombers during the trip. The fighters covering the bombers would have been either well above us or off to one side away from dropping bombs while they looked for the enemy; we saw none of those, either.

We had one short leg after the target and then a longer one that took us to the south of Brussels. There we descended to 14,000 feet. At 1540 I began to pick up GEE signals again and found we were about five miles south of track. I calculated a new course for the next leg, which took us to a point south of Ostende; and with numerous GEE fixes I was able to keep us on track all the way through this leg and the next section over the North Sea. On this leg we dropped down to 10,000 feet. We crossed the English coastline at Southwold and then proceeded in a northwest direction, over the mouth of the Wash, descending to 8,000 feet as we proceeded. We continued on up to Yorkshire and so back to base where we landed at 1732 hours, five hours and twenty-seven minutes after takeoff.

We were all tired, I suppose, from the strain as well as the work we had been doing. However, the raid was not at all what we had expected, and was almost an anticlimax after all of the thinking we had been doing beforehand and the images of guns firing, planes going down in flames, and so on. It had actually all been very peaceful with just a moment of apprehension when we saw the first puffs of anti-aircraft fire. We might have been on a training exercise for all of the excitement involved. However, it was good to be back on the ground with our first operational flight behind us.

* * *

Trucks took us back to the dispersal huts, where the debriefing took place. A senior officer from each of the trades was there: one for the pilots, one for the navigators, one for the bomb-aimers, and so on. The navigation officer looked over my logs and charts and asked a few questions and that was it.

I was tired. And although it had been cold during the flight, I was now on the ground in a warm hut still wearing my flying suit on top of my other clothing, and I felt hot, sweaty and dirty. As soon as the debriefing was over we went back to our billets, undressed and tumbled into bed with our minds reeling from the experience of the past few hours. Showers would have to wait until the morning. Now it was time for sleep, and in a few minutes I was gone.

After an op the debriefings were all verbal, but Min decided to keep some personal handwritten notes for himself. This was against the rules, but he hid them somewhere in his belongings and kept them as mementos of the war. Recently he turned these notes over to me and it is interesting to read what he had to say at that time. For Essen, his personal journal read:

> My first op. I wasn't scared during the morning. I thought I would be. They called us at 0730 hours, 0800 hours breakfast, 0930 hours main briefing. Everything of course was strange. After a couple it should be dead easy.

> Took off at 1200 hours. 10/10 S.C. [we were flying above a continuous layer of stratocumulus cloud] all the way there and back. I felt a bit shaky when we neared the target and I saw the smoke puff markers [coloured markers were placed above the clouds by the Master Bomber for us to use as aiming points since we could not see the actual targets on the ground] and puffs of flak [exploding anti-aircraft shells]. While the shells were aimed at us we could not hear the sound of the explosions over the roar of our own four engines. More in awe than fright though. Quite a sight. All the aircraft converging on one point. One thousand bombers on one city in 30 minutes! The squadron was carrying fifteen 500lb M.C. and G.P. [bombs] per aircraft.

> Expect to see big things in the paper tomorrow. Really uneventful. Saw only about a dozen flak puffs.

POST-ESSEN FLIGHT

After working for over five hours under a certain amount of tension I was tired, but exhilarated. I was greatly relieved to be back on the ground safe and sound, and I was satisfied that I had done the job for which I had been trained, and had not let the crew down. In the days ahead there was a new sensation of pride when entering the mess. I felt I was now part of the squadron, I no longer felt like an outsider, and I am sure I stood a little straighter and taller.

One final note about this and all subsequent ops: It did not matter at what time you landed, whether it was broad daylight or the dead of night. There was always a Salvation Army van on the tarmac with a Salvation Army officer standing beside it waiting to give you a cup of tea or a bun, or to just listen if you felt the need to talk to someone. The Sally Ann, as they were affectionately called, were and still are a wonderful organization doing a world of hands-on good, and I have always had a soft spot in my heart for them.

The day following the Essen raid, the *Daily Express* carried the headline, "KRUPPS WRITTEN OFF." In smaller print was,

> Last battle for Ruhr begins. Greatest RAF attack of the war hits Essen, arms city only 15 miles ahead of Monty's waiting armies. More than 1,000 RAF Lancaster and Halifax bombers made the greatest daylight air attack of the war yesterday by cascading about 4,500 tons of bombs on Essen in the Ruhr. It was all over in 30 minutes. The attack was controlled throughout by a master bomber and the bombers were covered by 200 fighters. At the same time 1,200 American bombers, protected by 750 fighters, plastered U-boat yards at Hamburg, Bremen and Kiel and oil refineries at Hamburg, Harburg and Bremen. Of the total American force of 1,950 planes only one bomber and three fighters failed to return.

All twenty-three bombers from 158 Squadron completed their mission and returned to base. Counting bombers and fighters, 3,150 planes had been involved in the operations that day. Amazing!

Once our training was over and we had started to fly on ops I thought there would be no one looking over my shoulder. How wrong I was! After all, I had navigated the plane to the target and back, reached the target when we were supposed to, and stayed close to track all the way. To the best of my knowledge I had done a good job.

Aerial photograph of Essen, taken in June 1945 after the end of the war, showing the destruction after numerous bombings. The ruined Krupps arms factory is in the centre of the photo.

W.R. Chorley, In Brave Company

It was accordingly somewhat of a surprise to have my log given back to me a few days later so that I could read the notes written on it by the navigation officer of C Flight, of which we were a part. They read:

> Work to the nearest half minute, this is quite accurate enough. Show W \ V's found in the Nav. Obs column and I suggest you show API readings in the General Column. Don't log turning points as Lat and Long, give them "letters." Try and squeeze your GEE a bit more. You can overcome the jamming by staying on Strobe Time Base. This is a good effort for your first trip. Keep it up."
>
> H E Forsdyke
>
> F/L C Flight

Our squadron flew to Essen eighteen times during the course of the war, putting up anywhere from four to twenty-four planes. Twenty planes were lost, and ten of these losses were incurred in 1942 and 1943 out of twenty-six planes! After the March 11th raid, a returning pilot noted in the debriefing that, "Nothing exceptional was seen."[2] He surely would not have made such a report during the grim days of 1942 and 1943.

---

[2] Statistics and quote taken from *In Brave Company* by W.R. Chorley (England: self-published, 1990), pp. 251-260.

DAILY EXPRESS

No. 13,969   MONDAY MARCH 12 1945   FOUNDED BY LORD B...RBROOK   Dim-out 7.37 p.m. to 7.0 a.m.   One Penny

LAST BATTLE FOR RUHR BEGINS: Grea... Essen, arms city only 15 miles ...ead of Monty's waiting armies   R.A.F. daylight attack of the war hits

KRUPPS WRIT'EN OFF

More than 4,000 tons: More than 1,000 planes

MORE than 1,000 R.A.F. Lancasters and Halifaxes made the greatest daylight air attack of the war yesterday by cascading about 4,500 tons of bombs on Essen, in the Ruhr.

This great R.A.F. assault was backed up by a force of 1,200 American "heavies" which plastered the U-boat yards at Hamburg, Bremen, and Kiel, and oil refineries at Hamburg, Harburg, and Bremen.

With the Allied armies standing on the Rhine less than 15 miles to the west, Essen is now a railway and communications centre of great importance to the enemy.

The objects of yesterday's attack were to write off Krupps, to make sure that the city cannot be used for industrial purposes, and to remove it as a supply point for the Germans in the west.

It was all over in 30 minutes. In that half-hour bombs plastered Krupps, the marshalling yards, and the inland docks.

The attack, covered by 200 fighters, was made through cloud, and was controlled throughout by a master bomber. Returning pilots reported that they saw smoke from large fires rising through the cloud to a great height.

100-mile fleet

As it flew out the great R.A.F. armada formed a mighty sky battle - fleet spanning the English countryside for more than 100 miles between the first and last planes.

Farmers in the fields, children at play in the lanes, villagers on their way to church stopped to listen as the great din of one of the engines of this great procession filled the sky

And pilots of one squadron said when they returned that Krupps and Essen must have received "a terrific plastering."

A total of 35,000 tons of bombs have been dropped on Essen during the war. It was first attacked on March 5, 1943, when it was one of the best-defended targets in Germany.

The attack opened the first major blow at the Ruhr. Yesterday's raid it is hoped, will mean the beginning of the last phase.

It is significant that this "best-defended target," yesterday presented almost no defence to our pilots. They reported that flak was particularly light, and that fighter opposition was non-existent.

Through cloud

The crews were directed by pathfinders and bombed by instruments. They reported that cloud was "ten-tenths," reaching 18,000 feet or so. but while it was impossible to see anything of Essen visually, smoke was seen rising more than 7,000 ...et.

At one station all but one of the squadron returned safely. Everyone waited tensely for the arrival of that one missing bomber ... was ... way to church. Then a message came ... "... for Charlie ... is safe ... own in France." She had dropped ...er bomb-load.

Comments by Flight-Lieutenant (Digger) Klemmer, of Adelaide, a 21-year-old Lancaster pilot, were typical of what most pilots had to say: "There cannot be very much left of Essen," he said. "Everything went according to schedule. It's given Essen and Krupps a knock."

The 1,200 American heavies that attacked Bremen and Hamburg were escorted by 750 fighters. Of the total American force of nearly 2,000 planes only one bomber and three fighters failed to return.

Article appearing in the *Daily Express* on March 12th, the day after the raid on Essen. Note the price of the newspaper!

Chapter 7

DORTMUND

The day following the raid on Essen, once more we found that our crew was to fly again. This time at the main briefing we found out that the target was Dortmund, a city on the east side of the Ruhr about twenty miles northeast of Essen. At this stage of the war Dortmund was finished as a manufacturing centre, but a great many highways ran through the city and it was used a great deal by the German army as a route for troops and supplies to the Rhine front or, in the case of retreat, as an escape route. The object of this raid, as some wag said, was "to resettle the bricks"—which would block the roads. Before the trip I saw an aerial photograph of a part of the city and he was correct. All you could see were the shells of buildings with a few walls standing! On the Essen trip the squadron had put up twenty-three planes, and for Dortmund twenty-four kites were scheduled to take part. Bomber Command had laid on 1,108 bombers as they continued to pulverize the Ruhr.

After the previous day's bewilderment we now knew what the drill was and didn't have to follow people around like sheep. After the main briefing we had our individual trade briefings.

We were beginning to enjoy the briefings given by the station's meteorological officer. He had an inordinate affection for his bicycle! He would carry it up onto the stage when it was his turn to brief the crews, and then when he was finished he rode it down the steps, bumpety, bump, and out a side door!

There were seventeen legs to this trip, so again I had a great deal of information to record at the top of my log at the briefing for the navigators. It might be worth mentioning here that in the RAF and RCAF each navigator was trained to operate on his own and was responsible for the navigation of his own aircraft. The result was always a loose gaggle of planes, all headed the same way, each under the direction of its navigator, who gave courses, air speed, heights, and so on to the pilot.

In the American air force the planes flew in formation and the navigator in the lead plane was responsible for the navigation of the whole formation, which would be made up of several planes. The lead navigator was accordingly well trained to do this and was more experienced and better trained than the remaining navigators in the formation. As a result, if the lead navigator were lost it created a problem—not insurmountable, but a problem nevertheless. The American planes were usually flying fortresses, and they were well named, as they had much more armament than we had. They had four or five gunners to our two; and flying in formation allowed the firing trajectories of each plane to overlap so that incoming fighters literally had to fly through a curtain of bullets.

Our route was much the same as the day before: down England to Reading, a run out to the middle of the Channel that took us about ten miles west of Brighton, then a leg into France just north of Abbeville, after which there were two legs taking us across France and Belgium. Then we turned northeast, crossing the Rhine about ten miles north of Cologne and skirting the densest part of the Ruhr straight into Dortmund. Once over water, the gunners checked their guns and reported to Min. While they were doing this you could hear the brief chatter of the guns over the roar of our four engines. You certainly felt more secure from enemy fighters when you heard the guns firing.

Over the Channel the wind speed and direction had changed enough from the information given us at base to put us about eight miles past the mid-Channel turning point. I calculated the new wind speeds and direction and gave the pilot the course and speed at which to fly over the next leg; this gradually got us back on course and along the track we were supposed to be following. You did not do such a correction with sharp turns because of the danger of colliding with other aircraft, but gradually changed course by a degree or two to make the correction. At 1530 hours, just before crossing the coast into the continent, the master bomb switch was turned off.

We were supposed to be on the target at 1639. At 1622 hours the master bomb switch was turned back on. At 1630 hours, thirty miles short of the target, the engineer commenced dropping window and kept this up until we were some fourteen minutes past the target. We had started at 5,000 feet and then, as we neared Dortmund, climbed to 18,000 feet, the height at which we were to bomb. At 18,000 feet you were usually above any clouds; and on a daylight raid the welcome sun created in you a sense of well-being as it bathed the aircraft around you in its light and sparkled on the metal.

At 1636 we began our bombing run and the bomb-aimer then directed the pilot until calling out, "Bombs gone!" at 1641. It was during the bombing runs that I had a minute or two to look out. I always wondered if I should do this, as I had no idea of what I might see; but curiosity always got the better of me. This time I saw no flak at all, only the coloured smoke puffs marking the aiming point that the planes were bombing above the cloud cover. Either I was improving or the Germans were having a bad day with their equipment to mess up our GEE system, as I was able to get GEE fixes most of the way to the target and very shortly after we turned for home.

Our route back to base took us parallel to the coast westward until we turned northwest across the edge of the North Sea making landfall at Southwold. At least now that the Allies were well into the continent, we did not have to worry about anti-aircraft fire on the entire trip over Europe. The next-to-final leg saw us cross the mouth of the Wash. The last short track was only of ten minutes' duration and took us straight into our base. We landed at 1921. We had flown 1,280 air miles and had been airborne for six hours and eight minutes. I had used up four pages for my log and 168 lines. That works out to a line each 2.2 minutes; and as the entries on a line varied from two notations to thirteen on some, it can be seen that all this paperwork, along with reading the various instruments used for navigation, plotting on my chart and calculating wind speeds, directions, and new courses, kept a navigator very busy. I was very tired at the end of this flight.

The navigation officer returned my log to me the following day to read his observations, and he had written on it: "Average trip. You were a bit late on target !!!" The three exclamation points were his. I looked at my chart and we had dropped our bombs at 1641 instead of 1639. I had been two minutes late! I really didn't think this made much difference in the midst of over 1,000 aircraft that formed a stream about 125 miles long!

In his personal journal Min said, in part,

> The whole op was almost identical to yesterday's. 1,070 bombers plus a couple of hundred fighters over the target area. Still very impressed with the kites around us. About half the flak of yesterday's raid. 15 five-hundred pound bombs per aircraft. Bombed smoke puff markers. Saw smoke billowing up 7,000 feet. Back about 1915 hours. Sure was worn out.

The paper reported the raid stating that nearly 5,000 tons had been dropped in blow number two of the Ruhr knockout. They also reported that while the raid was being carried out on Dortmund, the

DORTMUND

Nearly 5,000 tons go down in blow No. 2 of the Ruhr knock-out

Express Air Reporter

DORTMUND was hit yesterday by more than 1,000 Lancasters and Halifaxes with 5,000 tons of bombs. Nearly three-quarters of the force carried a 4,000-pounder in their load.

The city, although it has died as a major industrial centre, is a great transport hub. Nearly all troops and supplies bound for the front go through.

The attack was timed for 4.30 p.m., and, well before the main force reached the city the master bombers had directed the markers.

Aiming-point at the beginning of the attack was in the south of the city. For nearly half-an-hour the bombers, which stretched for 125 miles across the sky, concentrated there.

Then, just before five o'clock, the attack was switched to the centre of the city. High-explosive bombs were used to crater roads and railways and bring down on them those buildings still standing.

This attack brought the tonnage dropped on Dortmund to 20,000.

The Americans sent 650 heavies to devastate naval and military targets at the German Baltic port of Swinemunde, 35 miles north of Stettin—Red Army objective.

Another 750 raided six railway yards strung out east of the American trans-Rhine bridgehead at Remagen.

Losses were the lightest for many months.

Article appearing in the *Express* the day after the raid on Dortmund.

Americans sent 650 heavy bombers against the German Baltic port of Swinemünde and another 750 planes against six railway yards east of the American trans-Rhine bridgehead at Remagen. Losses were the lightest for many months.

In two days almost ten thousand tons of bombs had been dropped on Nazi Germany by the RAF—and the pasting was not over yet.

WUPPERTAL

After two ops in two days we were somewhat surprised to learn we were going on another on March 13th, this time to a city called Wuppertal. This city was almost straight south of Hagen and some miles to the south, southeast of the Ruhr complex. However, Bomber Command was pounding all the major centres to the east of the Rhine, and this city was to be no exception, although fewer planes took part.

The raid was almost identical to our first two ops and quite uneventful until we were on our way home. Twenty-two planes were laid on from our squadron and all returned home safely, as had been the case the previous two days. We were cooperating with the Allied armies and attacking marshalling yards to slow the enemy's retreat.

Airborne at 1252, it was twenty-two minutes later that we again set out, down England to Reading, and the usual track to the target. On the way in, our track took us over Charleroi in France and Liège in Belgium. We crossed the Rhine about five miles south of Düsseldorf and came at Wuppertal from the northeast. At 1601 I entered "bombs gone" in my log and we turned for home.

After the bombing run we turned onto a course that actually took us a little further into Germany in a southeasterly direction before turning onto another course that went almost straight south. Then we turned onto a southwesterly course to take us over the Rhine between Cologne and Bonn. The result of these legs meant that we stayed over German-occupied territory for more than the usual period. Before we got as far as the Rhine, we saw a puff of smoke behind us where an anti-aircraft shell had burst. These puffs continued to appear, steadily drawing nearer. Min started to fly a corkscrew, but no matter how he twisted and turned the puffs kept getting closer. It was a new type of gun that locked onto the target and kept correcting its aim no matter what you did. Just when it appeared the next couple of bursts would strike us, the puffs began to fall astern, gradually getting farther behind until they stopped altogether. Fortunately the gunners on the ground had not picked us up soon enough and we had flown out of range before the gun finished its job. It was a few minutes of heart-pounding excitement to see the shells bursting closer and closer. I don't know if Min reported this incident at the debriefing, but for some reason I did not enter it in my log.

We later passed over Brussels and flew at 8,000 feet most of the way home, descending to 4,000 feet as we neared Lisset. We joined the circuit over the station at 1817 hours and landed fourteen minutes later, having flown 1,252 air miles in five hours and thirty-nine minutes.

Forsdyke, the navigation officer, wrote "Average trip. OK." on my log. Perhaps he was busy that day, as he had no criticism of my work. (Then again, he may have been damning it with faint praise.)

Min's journal reported the following:

> For us the raid was almost identical to the first two. Actually a smaller effort, 300 bombers of 4 and 6 Groups with about the same [200-odd] fighter escort. Bomb load was 15 X 500 lb. MCs and GPs. Those fighter boys sure look comforting up there. Bombed through 9/10 stratocumulus. Gunners reported smoke on way out. Flak was very light. Same over Cologne. Uneventful.

As I was busy most of the time I never saw any of the fighter planes providing our escort, and German fighters were non-existent as far as we could see during the raids we had been on so far. These three ops had been almost like training exercises except for the little flak we had encountered, and none of that had been close to our plane. We were certainly feeling less apprehensive about flying on operations, and now that we had three under our belts we began to feel right at home back on base.

However, the war was not over yet, and in the days ahead we would find on one or two occasions that we were to receive a rude awakening!

* * *

From time to time, even near the end of the war, the Germans sent aircraft over at night to strafe Allied airfields and to try to generally create havoc and do all the damage they could, although even to the most hardened Nazis it must have been clear by now that they could not win the war.

The station at Lisset had been hit a couple of times and while we were stationed there a night attack occurred. John Prosser and I had been to the movies in Bridlington, and as we did not have a ride back to camp, we walked the long seven miles home. On the way, John sang as we trudged along, serenading the cows that looked curiously at us from the fields on either side of the road. It was the early hours of the morning when we arrived at the station and it was still abuzz with excitement about the night's events.

A number of low-flying German planes had followed the bomber stream back from a raid and shot up the station. The only evidence we saw of any damage was to one of the buildings where cannon shells had torn off some of the roof. Apparently no serious damage had been done, and no one had been hurt; but once the raid had ended and apprehension had dissipated there were some funny stories to be told.

The airman in charge of the van at the end of a runway had heard the planes and, expecting them all to be ours, turned on the runway lights. The next thing he knew, tracers were flying around his vehicle and he made an ignominious exit on the fly.

Around the airfield at certain intervals there were machine guns on posts. They had been put there years before in the event the station was attacked, either from the air or the ground. They were quite high and whoever was going to fire the guns sat on a seat partway up the post, similar to a seat you might find on a tractor. The seat was made of metal and was welded to the post.

A bomber was just landing when all hell broke loose. When the plane came to a halt, one of the gunners leaped out and tore over to one of the machine guns. He jumped up onto the seat and grabbed hold of the handles on the machine gun, but the seat and its attachments had rusted away over the years. The seat broke off and he found himself dangling down, hanging onto the handles, with the machine gun pointing straight up into the sky! He never got off one round.

That was the last such episode at 158 Squadron, and everyone was thankful it had not been the same as the one that occurred just before we arrived at the station, when people had been killed.

* * *

Across the road from 158 Squadron was a farm. In the field closest to the road the farmer kept a flock of sheep.

Two pilots on squadron approached the farmer and he agreed to sell them two of the sheep. He was to keep them with the rest of the flock, but they belonged to the officers. They had absolutely no intention of doing anything with the sheep, but they seemed to feel that owning the sheep put them in a class by themselves—sort of gentlemen farmers, a cut above their brother officers.

When time permitted, they walked across the road and stood by the fence. Sometimes they stood with one foot up on a rail and that gave them a sort of rustic look, as it was a pose the Yorkshire farmers often struck when surveying their animals. First there was a discussion to decide which were their two sheep. Then, when that was settled—probably quite incorrectly—they talked about whether the sheep would soon be ready for shearing, whether they should be bred to produce lambs, and other things about sheep that the farmer was himself probably mulling over.

When the war was over I did not hear what the two airmen did, but I suspect they went home without another thought about their sheep. The farmer was in pocket a few pounds, still had his two sheep, and probably thought the two officers were quite mad, or as he would tell his friends, "They were daft!"

* * *

One day we awoke to find a very dense low ceiling. The clouds could not have been more than a couple of hundred feet off of the deck. The powers that be wondered how thick the cloud cover was. If it was not too thick, some training could be done; but if it stretched up too high it would be dangerous to try flying. They needed someone to go up and have a look, and guess who volunteered? That man certainly loved to fly!

We got suited up and into the plane and off we went. Min steadily climbed higher and higher but the clouds were still as thick as ever and he decided it was time to turn back. He had been flying straight after leaving the base and to get back home he now flew a sort of square, making three left turns that should bring us back over base in line with the runway. I had not been navigating, as we would never be far from the station.

Lower and lower we went, and suddenly we were under the clouds and there in front of us was the runway. We were on a perfect approach. I can't remember the exact words that were spoken, but Min came in for some congratulations for a perfect flight.

Min landed the plane and once on the ground things seemed a little different. They were different because we had landed at another air force station! In those days, England was carpeted with flying fields and this one was apparently only a few miles from our own. Min taxied around the perimeter and took off. This time to offset the wind, which had blown us farther than expected, Min flew a longer leg on the reverse course. We were in cloud again but when we descended and broke out into the clear we were again in line with a runway, this time our own.

Min reported that the cloud was too thick for flying but I am not sure if he reported that we had landed at another base. He is still not saying!

FRIDAY THE 13TH

On the 29th of February 1944, a Mark III Halifax was delivered directly from the Handley Page factory to an airfield at Leconfield. On March 10th it was transferred to Lisset, where it was to be held in reserve. However, when one of 158 Squadron's planes crashed in Belgium this new aircraft was pressed into service.

Its first operational flight was to Nürnberg, and shortly thereafter it was given the name *Friday the 13th*. In spite of such a name, it proved to be very lucky for a number of crews, seeing some finish a complete tour on its wings.

The plane's last op was to Wangerooge on April 25th, 1945, its 128th operational flight. It had been damaged by flak three times, survived a number of attacks by enemy fighters, and had had to abort only three missions due to mechanical difficulties.

Friday flew 550 hours, a remarkable achievement, thanks to the skill of the men who flew in her and the ground crew who kept her fit for the next flight.[3]

The legendary *Friday the 13th*.

W.R. Chorley, In Brave Company

[3] Ibid., p. 286.

Chapter 8

On Wednesday the 14th of March we were very surprised to find Min's name was again on the duty roster, as we had already flown three times in three days. There was just one difference with this op. It was at night.

Since time began man has been afraid of the dark. Perhaps there has been a deep-seated fear in his psyche from time immemorial, when in the darkness it was hard to defend himself against a wild animal or an enemy because of the element of surprise. Whatever the reason, man has always tried to surround himself with light when the sun has gone down, and he rejoices when it returns.

I am sure there was a feeling of apprehension in the crew, and that this op would somehow be different. I know this is how I felt. We were already tired from the three previous trips, but no one mentioned this or spoke about any fears they might have. We had a job to do and we just got on with it.

It would not be too bad for me, as I simply had to draw the blackout curtains in front of my workstation and turn on a light by which I would work. Min would have to be even more alert, as he would not have the comfort of seeing dozens of planes all around us flying in a loose formation to the target. They would be there, somewhere in the darkness, but where? Too close? Is that shadow a fighter? There would be a much greater danger of collision. He would have to pay more attention to the instruments, as he could not see the horizon; and he would have to keep a sharp eye out to the front in case we were overtaking anyone, or if another plane was veering into our path at close range. Worst of all, the gunners would not be able to see attacking planes at a distance; they would be right on us before we would have a chance to react. All they could do was strain their eyes to peer into the darkness, ready to sound the alarm in an instant. The tension they would be under would be intense. If we were attacked, the first indication they would most likely have would be incoming tracers!

By now we were used to the drill: a main briefing, separate trade briefings, a shower, a meal; and then if there was time, a nap before donning our flying suits and being driven in trucks to the aircraft.

The target this time was Homburg, another city in the Ruhr. The reason for the raid was tactical, which I suspect at this stage of the war simply meant rearranging the rubble in the city to obstruct retreating Germans! It was the usual flight down England to Reading, across the Channel, and then west to the target. There were twenty different legs to the track this time, so I had a great many spaces to fill in on my log before we even got off the ground— 280, to be exact!

After settling down at my desk in the aircraft, the first entry in my log was made at 1650 hours, when I turned on the instruments by which I would navigate. I set the dead reckoning device to the base coordinates, loaded the Very pistol, and made a few other checks. We were airborne at 1719.5 and climbed to 7,000 feet, joining the circuit of circling planes. At 1737 we crossed over base and set course on the first leg of our trip. We had started thirty seconds ahead of schedule.

We did our usual run on a course of 268 degrees until we crossed over the upper estuary of the Humber River. There we altered course to 185 degrees for a straight run to Reading, the point where we would again alter course to cross the Channel into Europe. The wind speeds and directions I calculated were much the same as those that had been forecast, and so we never strayed more than a mile or two off track. As we were travelling at a ground speed of 200 knots, this meant that at worst we were just forty seconds away from track—a minor adjustment if it became necessary.

At 1847 we crossed the coastline just a few miles west of Brighton. Now an event occurred that made things even more harrowing. Up to this point, all of the aircraft had had their navigation lights on, a green light on the starboard side and a red light on the port side. These lights were not particularly bright, but at night you could spot them for miles. Now, as we came closer to the enemy, they were turned off! Immediately all the planes whose lights you could see before disappeared in the darkness. Now it became even more crucial for Min and the gunners to be alert.

At mid-Channel we again altered course, crossing into Europe several miles northwest of Dieppe. At 1853 the bombs were fused and the order in which they would be dropped selected. The gunners had previously tested their guns over the Channel. They made quite a racket over the roar of the engines, but fortunately Min gave the gunners the order, so you were warned in advance there would be a test, and knew it was not an attack.

We passed over Amiens and continued generally eastward toward the Ruhr, changing course only as we entered another leg. We were running a minute or so late, and so at 1943 I asked Min to increase the airspeed from 182 to 192 knots. We were to bomb from a height of 13,000 and had to climb from 7,000 feet, the height at which we had flown until now. During the climb our airspeed dropped off to 172 knots and by my calculations we were again running late. Ernie took over for the bombing run and at the same time I asked Min to increase the airspeed to 202 knots. Ernie sang out "Bombs gone" at 2033.5, and I entered this in the log with some satisfaction as that was our precise time on target.

We had a short leg to the north and then turned back to the west. This kept us clear of the bombers still approaching the target. I had been able to get GEE fixes right up to the start of the bombing run, but then lost the signal, and it was some thirty minutes later before I could obtain another fix. However, we were right on track and no course correction was necessary. At 2120 we ceased dropping window. After bombing at 13,000 feet we had dropped down to 9,000 and then 5,000 feet before again climbing to 7,000 feet, at which level we flew the rest of the way home. My chart gets a bit confusing for the latter part of the trip, as the track home was virtually along the same line as the track out from the middle of France to Reading and back up England, so a lot of the recorded info was overlapping.

At 2202 Ernie checked for any hang-ups of the bomb load, which he always did on the way home, and finally at 2325 we were over base and landed at 2332.5. We had covered 1,092 air miles and been in the air for six hours and fifteen minutes. Thank goodness for youth and strong bladders! Min, who could not have left his position in any event, had a tin and a tube running to it, but never had to use it!

There were the usual debriefings when the navigation officer went over my log and chart. Little was said at that time, but eventually you were given your log to read the comments thereon. This time I was told I should have checked some of the equipment more frequently and I had again forgotten to letter all turning points! At least we had returned safely and our first night trip, with its attendant worries, was now behind us.

The Squadron sent out seventeen planes on this raid. Sixteen completed the mission, but one returned to base without dropping its bombs. When this happened it was usually due to malfunction of equipment.

Min's personal journal for Homburg reads:

> My first night op. Target—marshalling yards, industrial area. Load, 15 x 500 lb. G.P. and M.C. Ground target indicators through light haze. Very straightforward. Naturally much more colourful than "daylights." Flak light. Fighters followed our stream home and put down some amber flares over England. Height 13,000 feet. 270 aircraft.

HAGEN

On March 15th we found out that we were scheduled to fly another op, again at night, and at the main briefing we were told the target was Hagen, in the Ruhr. This was our fifth day in a row of flying on ops and we were getting very tired. I guess we were all shocked, as it seemed the constant flying and the stress related to the trips would never end. However, the adrenalin continued to flow, and once the proceedings began at the main briefing we stayed alert until we hit the sack hours later. In a recent poem I wrote about Gallipoli, I wrote, "The pulse races when bugles blow." This flight turned out to be the hairiest one yet.

Our track took us again straight down England to Reading, a slight turn to port to take us to the middle of the Channel, a further turn to port to bring us over the French coast, and then a long leg to a point about thirty miles south of Brussels. We then were to turn onto a northeast course as though we were heading to the north of the Ruhr; but at the German border, a swing to the southeast and a further change of course to take us between Cologne and Bonn brought us to a point thirty miles almost directly south of Hagen. After the run up to Hagen we were to turn for home, the track missing the major centres of the Ruhr. We were to meet up with the track used going in when we were just back into Belgium and from there follow the outward bound track to the French coast, a slightly eastern route across the Channel, again to poor old Reading and so up England to base.

This was our second op at night and there was always a feeling of apprehension for the rest of the crew when they could not see what was in the air around them unless it was extremely close. This was particularly hard on the air gunners' nerves as they continually searched for incoming fighters. I was of course busy at my plotting table and, although I was not looking out, I was aware of the strain on everyone from the voices over the intercom. Once or twice on night ops a gunner would tell the pilot to start a corkscrew manoeuvre when he thought he saw something; and whether we were attacked or not, we did not sustain any damage. The gunners would be excited and start chattering on the intercom until Min told them to keep quiet and report only when they had something to say. These episodes lasted only a minute or so and then everything would calm down again; but when they did happen, I am sure my heart rate speeded up when the sudden order from the gunner to corkscrew was given.

We were airborne at 1713 hours and set out on our first leg at 1726, one minute ahead of schedule. I was able to obtain GEE fixes all the way to the target and the bomb-aimer sang out, "Bombs gone!" at 2035, bang on schedule. I had a course ready to give Min one minute after the bombs had been dropped and we were clear of the target area.

When we turned onto a course of 265 I was still having my usual look out the window and there, about forty miles dead ahead, was a terrible sight. Some thirty or more searchlights lit up the sky at the Rhine directly in our path. You could see bombers silhouetted against the glow, and some were coned by more than one searchlight. I saw one plane on fire and then had to get back to work; but the thought of heading straight through that mess was enough to make your stomach churn.

The first fix I obtained, we were well to the south of track. I thought I must have made a mistake and quickly got a second fix that showed we were even farther away from where we were supposed to be. I asked Min what course he was flying and he told me. It was not the course I had given him and it was leading us steadily away from the main stream. I could not fault Min. He was looking straight at all of those searchlights, which we were rapidly approaching, and rather than run the gauntlet he turned to one side.

Unfortunately the course he was on was taking us straight into Düsseldorf, a major German city. I began giving Min courses as fast as I could get new GEE fixes, and also some general instructions telling him to turn twenty degrees to port or a certain number of degrees to starboard. I gradually eased us around the south side of Düsseldorf, and then using the H2S screen tried to avoid as many of the built-up areas as I could. We must have awakened a few people as we passed over or around these areas, as searchlights would suddenly come on looking for us; but always, fortunately, just after we had gone by. I guess they wondered what a lone aircraft was doing over their town!

After crossing the Rhine I plotted a track about ten miles south of Gladbach and then a new course to get us back into the main bomber stream. By this time the searchlights were long since behind us, and amazingly enough we were only one minute behind schedule in spite of our detour.

The evening was not over yet. Night fighters were out in force, and it is possible one or two of the gunners' warnings were for real. The fighters followed the main stream back to a point south of Reading and when one of the crews from 158 Squadron became aware of this infiltration, as the German fighters dropped flares to try and spot bombers below them, they diverted to land at Pershore, an intruder diversion base.

Min saw a bomber shot down by fire pointing upward, and we later learned that some German fighters had been equipped with a platform on top of the aircraft with machine guns or cannon pointing upward. They then slid underneath an unsuspecting bomber and fired straight up into the plane. The German code name for this kind of attack was "*Schlagen Musik.*" *Schlage* means "hit" or "strike," and can also mean "punish"; so that the guns firing upward were "punishment music."

The wireless operator had his "Fishpond" screen to watch, and on this trip he kept a close eye on it. Later, on the trip home, a rocket was fired at us from the ground and passed in front of us and then exploded with no damage done. We landed at base at 2333 hours. We had flown 1,259 air miles and been airborne for six hours and twenty minutes.

Min's official report read in part as follows:

> At 2100 hours, flying at 12,000 feet, just south of Genk, Belgium, whitish or yellow upward tracer was seen 1,000 to 2,000 yards away on our starboard bow and an unidentified aircraft then burst into flames and exploded in the air. Earlier when east of Neuss, a red rocket, leaving a slight trail, shot toward our aircraft from starboard and passed ahead. It exploded and then continued its flight before finally dying out.[4]

His personal journal told a somewhat different story!

> Target was built-up areas, communications, troops armour. A fine raid. Load: one 2,000-pound cookie, 11 incendiary clusters. Total weight, 8,500 pounds. Cloud 3 to 8,000 feet over French coast and the way back home.

---

[4] Ibid., p. 210

Target clear. Height 20,000. 277 aircraft plus fighter escort to target. Lots of light flak below us. Good run up and should have been a good prang. We were last wave. Saw lots of fire. Saw some 30 searchlights that were laid about on track required. Turned onto a course to avoid these. Must have held it too long and found ourselves 090 from Düsseldorf, making straight for it [which would have been suicide for a single aircraft]. Bob gave me courses around the south side of Düsseldorf—easier than getting back on track. Probably saved our bacon. On regaining track had to dodge the odd searchlight and finally a rocket. Both were more a scare than danger.

At about 0600 East saw one of our kites shot down by vertical tracer. (Found out on debriefing that a fighter with guns pointing up creeps up underneath you and—!)

We lost seven kites on the do, two of which we know were shot down by our own A.A. over Belgium. One of our squadron boys was opened up on but got out OK.

Jerry fighters followed us in over the coast of England and dropped amber flares.

Absolutely tired out after five consecutive days of operations. Except in special "dos" the maximum is two!!

I expected I would get a blast from the navigation officer when I turned in my log and chart at the debriefing, but he merely said that I had had a "different trip," or words to that effect. When I got my log back to scan a day or two later, two officers had signed it with each putting in his own remarks. One said, "Good trip. Tracking etc. above average." The other said, "A very good trip. I'm pleased to see you agree with our system and proving it works very well. Try astro compass checks." Not a word about our getting off course. Amazing!

The next day I handed Min a printed, handwritten note to the effect that if he was going to ignore the course given to him by his navigator he should at the very least let his navigator know! Fortunately such a situation never arose again.

The following night we suffered our first casualty. It was not caused by bullets but was brought on by the war in general and our work in particular. Our rear gunner, the placid Yorkshire farm boy, had heart palpitations and a nervous breakdown, and he was shipped off to hospital. We did not see him again. Apparently the strain of peering out into unfriendly skies, especially at night, for five days and nights straight had been too much for him. It was a

Hagen raid: portion of my log. Shows entries from 2015 to 2120 hours, covering the period from just before the bombing run until we were back with the main stream after our lonely trip around Düsseldorf and Gladbach.

Author

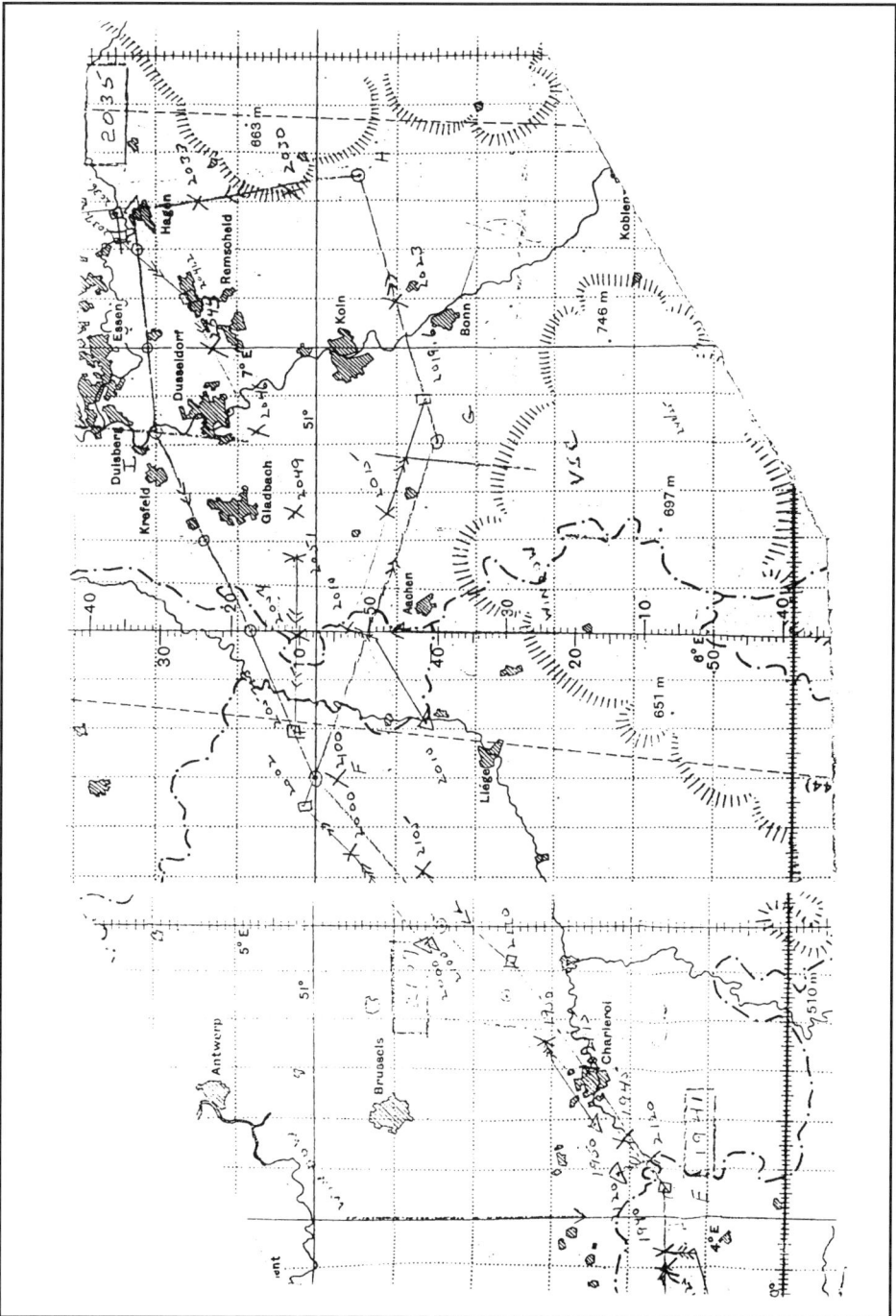

Hagen raid: portion of my chart. Shows the approach to the target well south of the Ruhr, our detour after leaving Hagen around the south side of Düsseldorf and Gladbach and, after regaining the stream, our flight back through Belgium.

Author

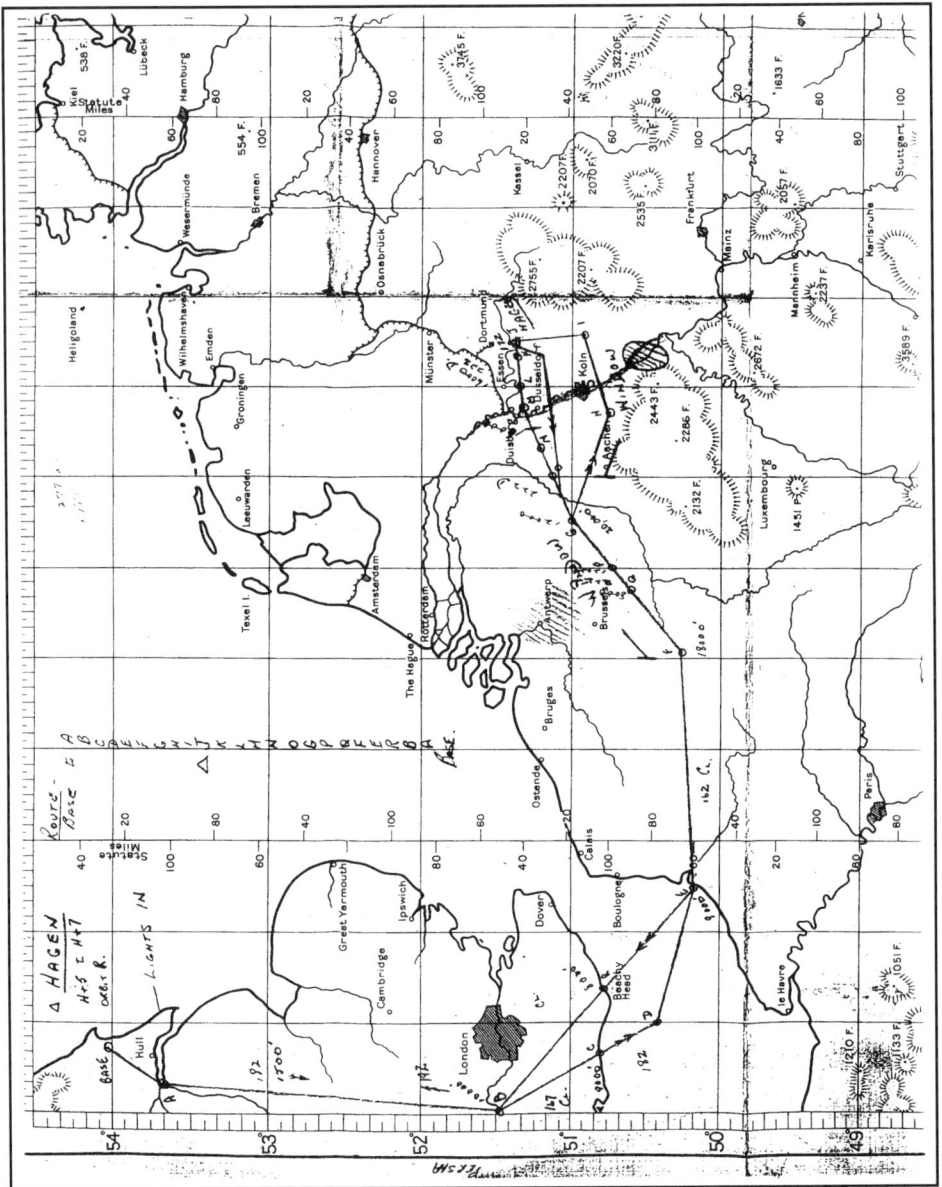

Min's own map of the trip to Hagen. Note the detour around Düsseldorf!

Menno Bartsch

good thing I had so much to do at my job; it is hard to say how I would have felt in his shoes. Another rear gunner was assigned to us, a Canadian with the rank of Warrant Officer 2, by the name of Jack Mino.

After five straight days on operational flights we were exhausted, both physically and mentally, and we welcomed a short leave. I headed for Trowbridge.

* * *

Some of the people in the British Isles who had larger homes opened them up to entertain the troops on weekends or when they had short leaves. They would host one or two men, whom the family would treat royally; and it was a lovely change from staying in camp when you had a forty-eight-hour pass.

Min and Ernie had put their names in for such a weekend and they visited a dentist and his family who lived in the town of Croxdale, Durham. They enjoyed a couple of such visits, and one weekend for a change I went with Ernie when Min was off to London.

When not eating in the dining room or in our bedrooms sleeping, most of our time was spent in the glorious living room. It was huge and had several groupings of furniture in it. To one side was a grand piano, which I had fun playing. Two or three clusters of comfortable and straight-backed chairs were placed around the room, the largest being in front of the huge fireplace. However, the main attraction was the long west wall, which was all glass and looked out over a narrow greenhouse. The greenhouse overlooked a garden. There were three doors out, one at either end and one in the middle. Through the middle door you looked down a pathway covered by a trellis on which roses intertwined and bloomed.

The house had central heating, but strange as it may sound, you could not operate the furnace if you could not drive a car! You left the house and walked around to the garage, which was built in to one side of the house. Then you backed the car out of the garage. Underneath the spot where the car had stood was a trap door that you pulled up, revealing some steps that led down to a tunnel. You walked along the tunnel for several feet and there stood the furnace. While this seems an odd way to have the heating set up, it had its practical side, as the dirt and grime connected with the operation of the furnace was kept away from the rest of the house.

One of the dentist's daughters, whose husband was in the army in the Middle East, entertained us by showing us the sights of

Durham. We went boating on the river with swans swimming along beside us; toured Durham Cathedral; and attended a play, *George the Third*, starring Robert Morley. It was a wonderful holiday; and in the evening, sitting by the crackling fire, the war seemed far away.

Some time after this holiday there was a party at the mess on our station. There were groups of entertainers who went about putting on shows to cheer you up, and one was visiting 158 Squadron. We invited the dentist's daughter who had been kind to us down to Bridlington to see the show. She stayed at a hotel and Min, Ernie and I chipped in and paid her train fare and for the room.

The show apart from some songs was all comedy, but for the first little while no one laughed. Finally the action was halted and one of the performers came to the front of the stage. He said that British humour was different from what we were used to in North America, but that was all right, they understood this; but he asked for our patience, and sure enough it was not very long before we were all howling with laughter.

I can remember one gag that ran through the whole program. A fellow dressed as an airman entered the stage from one side and exited at the other. He was carrying an empty specimen bottle and he smiled as he looked at the audience. A little later after one or two skits he again walked across the stage. He had taken off his tie and jacket and looked a little concerned. The bottle was still empty. This kept up throughout the revue until on his last walk across the stage he was in his underwear. He was crying uncontrollably and the bottle was still empty!

After the show the troupe joined us in the mess for drinks and conversation. It was a great change from the usual routine.

Chapter 9

WITTEN

On Mar. 19th, after a four-day rest, Min's name again turned up for duty. This was to be a night trip and the target was Witten, a city at the southwestern corner of the Ruhr complex. As well as high explosives, we were to carry incendiary clusters, as the object was to flatten the town. It was said to be still pretty well intact and it was being used heavily as an escape route by the German army. Anything to block the roads would help the cause.

We took off at fifty-two minutes after midnight and were on course for our first leg one minute later. This was our third night op in a row; we did not know it at the time, but it was to be our last night operation before the war ended.

As per usual we flew south to Reading, turned southeast, avoiding London by a wide margin, across the Channel and across France and Belgium. Just north of Liège we began flying in a northerly direction and crossed the Rhine well north of the Ruhr. With some ten minutes left to target, we turned straight for Witten and I recorded "bombs gone" at 0415, a minute ahead of schedule.

We bombed from 17,000 feet. There were a lot of scattered searchlights and on our way out of the target area one of the gunners sang out "Corkscrew!" As we broke away, the attacking plane was identified as a Junkers 88. It scored no hits nor did our gunners. When the request for a corkscrew was given, Min reacted instantly and I had little time to grab my navigating tools to stop them from falling off my plotting table before hanging on for dear life as the plane went through its violent turns and ups and downs in the manoeuvre. The gunners were firing away and you could hear the chatter of the guns above the roar of the engines. Their fire must have been accurate enough, as they lost sight of the fighter, which broke away from the attack.

This occurred at 0418; and at 0511 we were again attacked twice, the first indication each time being the shout of a gunner followed by the plane lurching to one side as Min took the plane into a turning dive. Min instituted corkscrews each time and on the second such manoeuvre, when we were again followed by a plane, Min told the gunners to shoot at him. They had been holding off as they had not identified the aircraft and thought it might be one of ours. They opened fire and the fighter broke away, but then surprisingly it fired off red flares before disappearing. This was the first trip on which we had been attacked in close by fighter planes and fortunately it was the last. Anti-aircraft shells exploding were one thing, but another plane, much faster than your aircraft, coming at you firing cannons with a view to shooting you out of the sky was another. It was heart-stopping to say the least; and when the attack was over, you were still wondering where he was and whether he would be back.

The rest of the flight was uneventful and we more or less traced our track out to get home. However, we did skirt London more closely and it was a good thing we did not stray off course over that city or we would have had a warm welcome! We reached base at 0715 and landed at 0724.

During this op, after all the criticism I had been getting I worked very hard at filling in all the spaces in my log. I even recorded data I had not done on previous trips, such as bombs fused and selected, master bomb switch off, all exterior lights checked out, windowing commenced, the start of the bombing run, the hang-up check, nav lights off and nav lights on. I was never more than two or three miles off track at any point and managed to get GEE fixes all the way there and back. My work was rewarded; when I got my log back to see the comments, which bore the Toogood signature, they read, "Good trip. Plenty of work done. Good tracking." However, he could not resist one tweak and added that I could have made more compass checks!

Min's personal journal read as follows:

> Height 17,000 feet. Load, one 1,000-lb, two 500-lb plus 10 incendiary clusters for a total of 8,000 lbs. Target was supposed to be the last upright town in the Ruhr. Due to bombing of other targets, importance as communications centre has grown. Object was to flatten the town, not the civilians! 300 aircraft and 70-odd fighters.
>
> Bags of searchlights, mostly scattered on way in. Over target at 0415. We were nearly the first to bomb. No master bomber. Followed out of target by Ju 88 as identified on breakaway after my corkscrew. Followed again by an aircraft. Two sets of corkscrews. Gunners took a shot at him when he followed us through the last one. About 200 rounds each gun, that is, 1,600 rounds. He broke away and fired red flares. Might have been one of our own fighters—damned fool if he was! Landed about 0715 in daylight.

After debriefing and a meal it was off to bed, and I doubt many minutes elapsed before we were all sound asleep. We had been up all night and after a flight of six hours and thirty-five minutes, accompanied at all times with the roar of the engines, the strain of the fighter attacks and in my case the steady work at my table, your mind became numb and it would not be until you woke up that all would fall into perspective. For now it was blessed oblivion.

Robert C. Kensett, Flying Officer J 40819. Officer and gentleman, age 21, fully trained and with several operational flights under his belt.

Author

* * *

It was almost a tradition for the aircrews on squadron to remove the wire band from the inside of their caps so that the crown folded down slightly at the sides. We certainly did not want to look like sprogs (green aircrew), so we followed suit.

It is interesting to observe the difference between the caps of the British and American top brass. Leigh–Mallory, who was British, was the air commander-in-chief for the invasion. He wore a cap with the wire still in and it sat straight on the top of his head and looked as though it was stiff as a board. Leigh–Mallory was very formal, pessimistic and indecisive and was not much liked.

On the other hand, General Elwood (Pete) Quasada, the American commander of the close support squadrons, wore a hat that looked as though he had folded it up and kept it in his pocket for a week! He was gregarious, decisive and not averse to going up to the front lines and crawling around in the mud to see how effective his crews were in supporting the infantry.

I wonder if it is possible to divine a person's character from a study of his hat?

GLADBECK

Back at Lisset, on March 24th, our crew was again called upon with twenty-one other crews to fly to Gladbeck, a city on the north side of the Ruhr city complex. The purpose of the raid was said to be tactical, which meant the whole town, troop concentrations in the town, and the communication systems.

This was a daylight operation and there were the usual briefings and other activities that occupied our time before takeoff, with which we were now well acquainted. We were airborne at 0913, joining a stream of some 250 bombers at 0923. The route was the usual one for the Ruhr, down to Reading, altering course across the Channel, and through France and Belgium. Just west of Liège we turned northeast, which took us level with the north end of the Ruhr cities, and then ten minutes from Gladbeck we altered course straight toward the target. At 1302.5 I noted in my log "bombs gone," two-tenths of a minute after the time we had been given back at base. Surely the nav officer could not complain about that and say I was late again!

We saw no enemy fighters, and flak was very light; but our crew saw one plane hit, which Min saw on fire and it exploded before crashing. Our return track was straight back to the coast and up over the North Sea to base, where we landed at 1505 after flying nearly six hours, having travelled 1,238 air miles. The plane that went down was piloted by Warrant Officer Yeoman. Three survived, but Yeoman and the rest of the crew were lost. These were the last airmen killed from 158 Squadron during the war.[5]

My log was again marked by Toogood, and he did not like it. The log had numerous question marks all over it and his report read:

> Your chart is far more presentable than your log. When
> you alter course fill in all the necessary columns. Even if
> you are following the stream, log the courses you are

---

[5] Ibid., p. 210

flying and work out ETAs for yourself. You are there to navigate your aircraft, not just relax and blindly follow someone ahead. Check your compasses every 20 minutes, not twice during the whole trip. This is not the standard which can be expected of you.

AVERAGE.

Of course I had not been blindly following the plane ahead, but steadily feeding courses to Min. However, you had no opportunity to complain—not that you would have even if you had had the chance. You just had to swallow your pride and take whatever criticism they dished out. You did not know how the other navigators fared and you did not ask. I wonder now what remarks appeared on Toogood's or Forsdyke's logs when they were active on ops in the days gone by!

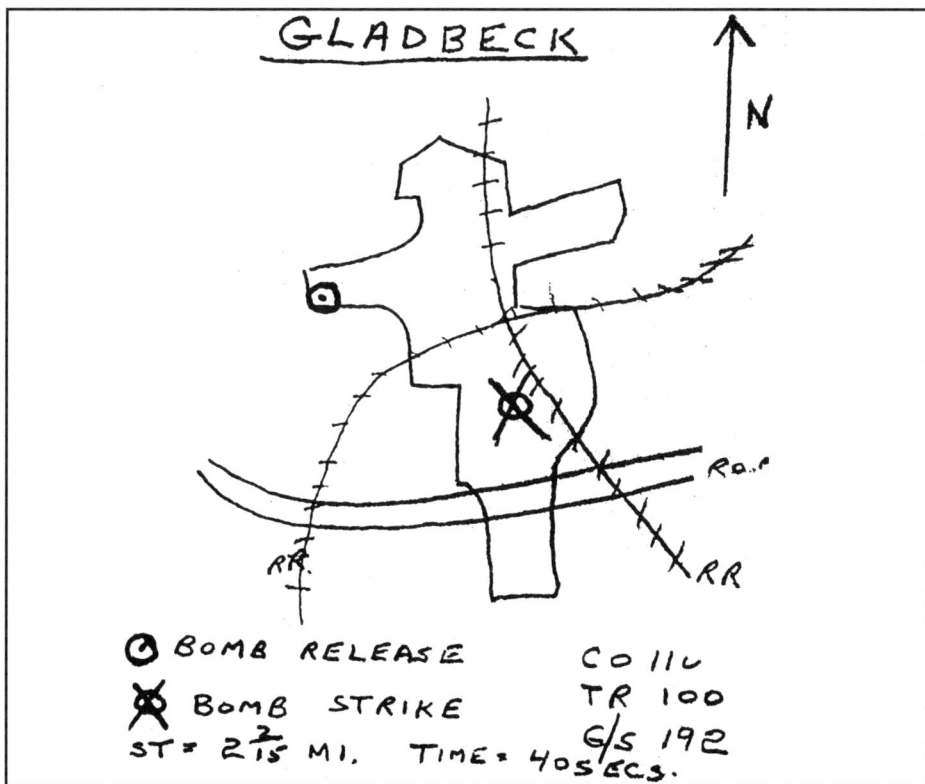

Hand-drawn map of part of Gladbeck, showing where bombs were released and where they struck, as well as two railroad lines and a road. The bombs hit two and two-fifteenths miles beyond the point at which they were released after an interval of forty seconds. (There is just one thing wrong with this drawing: it shows we were flying southeast, whereas we were flying northwest when we dropped the bombs! The bomb-aimer may have drawn this from the pictures he took after releasing the bombs and somehow got a reverse view.)

Ernie Pollitt

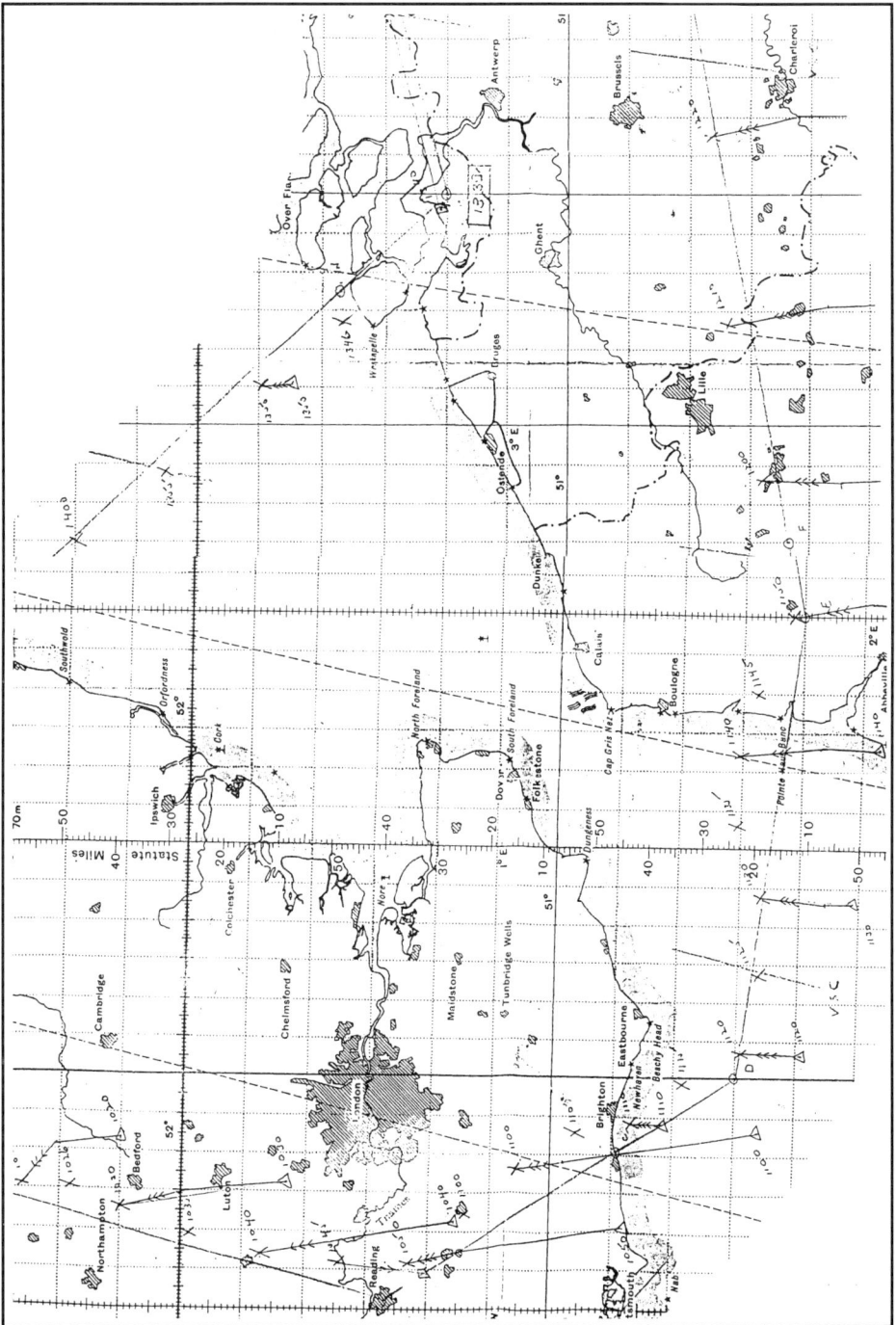

Chart of flight to Gladbeck. Note that trip was planned to reach target without crossing built-up area of the Ruhr.

Author

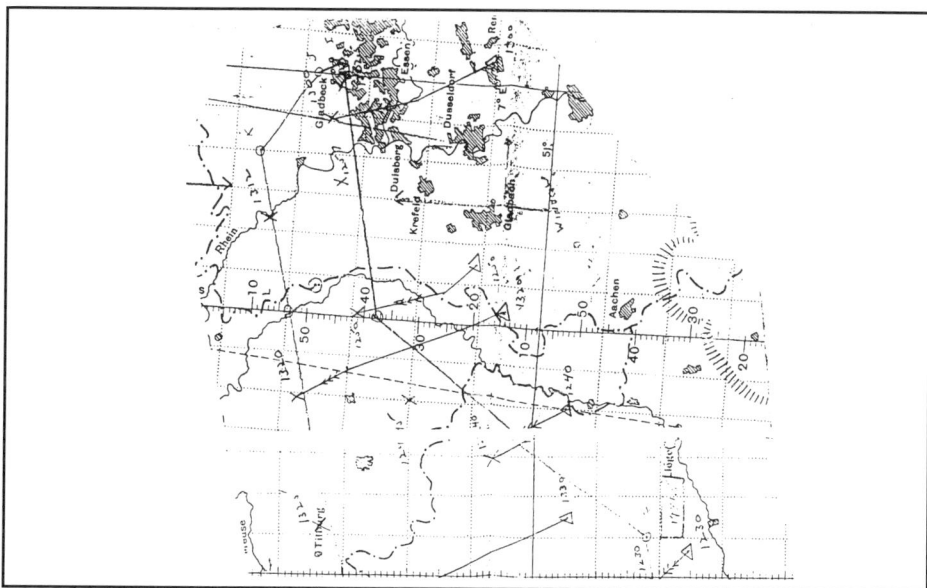

Chart of flight to Gladbeck.

Min's personal journal read as follows:

Height 18,000 feet. Load, 14 x 500 lb for a total of 7,000 pounds. 250 aircraft. Master Bomber controlled. Gaggle formation. Visibility about 20 miles. Target was the town in general and communications. Army assistance. Saw the smoke screen on the Rhine west bank. Flak was very light but one of our crews in "Q" caught a packet. The boys saw one parachute open. I saw the aircraft spiral down under our kite, the whole trailing edge of its main plane ablaze. It blew up before it hit. Over our target at 13:02.5. Had spare gunner (tail) WO2 Jack Mino, a Canadian, substituting for Sgt. Southwell, who had been taken off ops for a weak heart and nerves. ("Q" was a section of the planes from 158 Squadron. We were in "X.")

* * *

MÜNSTER

On Mar. 25th, the day after the raid on Gladbeck, we found ourselves again on another op, this time to the city of Münster. Münster was some forty miles to the northeast of the Ruhr valley and was not in a complex of cities as was the Ruhr. It was a major centre through which the Germans were withdrawing their armies eastward. The railway yards were said to be our target, although clobbering the entire city was more likely the objective, in order to clog the streets with rubble and so hold up the Germans' retreat.

By now we had the drill down pat: our mandatory shower, the greasy meal of bacon and eggs, and the ride out to the aircraft. We were again flying in X-Xray. Min as usual examined the bomb bay and gave his ritual slap to the HE bomb in the centre, after which we all clambered aboard. Previously at the navigation briefing I had filled in the top part of my log with the info provided and as there were only fifteen legs on our route I had only 180 squares to fill in!

It was an early daylight op and we were airborne at 0735 hours, climbing to 6,000 feet. This time our route was different in that we started from Flamborough Head, a headland a few miles north of base, where we joined the bomber stream, flew south to just north of the Humber River, where we turned southeast and flew over the North Sea to the island chain off the coast of southern Holland. There we turned due east and flew to a point some forty miles west of the Rhine, where we again turned onto a course straight for Münster. Over the North Sea the gunners had tested their guns and found them to be in order.

I was some twelve miles off track, having used the wind speed and direction given us on the ground; but as the track on which our plane was heading intersected the next leg, I waited until then to give Min a new course rather than trying to get back on track earlier. After that GEE fixes showed us dead on track the rest of the flight, proving my own calculations of wind speeds and directions were correct.

Up until this point it had all been routine, but when Ernie took over for the bombing run it was a different story. The engineer had been tossing out window for some minutes and once we began our bombing run, I had my usual few minutes to look out my small window before giving Min the new course that I had already calculated for the next leg.

We were bombing from 17,000 feet and this time the Germans had the range down pat. At our height over the target there were dozens—perhaps hundreds—of anti-aircraft shells bursting, and it was obvious that the enemy were trying to protect the railway yards and the city as best they could. The railways and roads were of vital importance for withdrawal of the German armies as the Allies advanced eastward.

The sky seemed to be full of grayish-brownish puffs of smoke, and each puff represented a bursting shell. They were all around us and near misses shook the aircraft. My feet were resting on the floor and it felt as though someone were hitting the soles of my feet, hard, with a piece of wood! For the first time on any flight I was frightened. It was an odd fear. I did not really think of being hurt or killed. My fear seemed to be directed toward the fact that the aircraft might be disabled or shot down. Our plane was our safe haven in the sky. The roar of its engines was a comforting sound. Inside it we felt invulnerable and the thought of losing that protection was intolerable. My parachute was stowed under my seat and once the plane began to toss from the concussions I kept one hand on it, ready to clip it on in the event Min gave the order to bail out. That was the only flight on which I did this and I kept hold of my chute until we were clear of the area.

The rear gunner could only see what we had passed through and not what was coming. The rest of the crew could only sit and pray. Ernie was busy with the bombing run and was concentrating on his job, singing out: "Left . . . right . . . steady." He had to put outside distractions out of his mind and to his credit he did, finally announcing "Bombs gone" at 1019, thirty seconds ahead of our time on target.

It was far worse for Min, who could see the area of bursting shells ahead and had to fly directly into the maelstrom, turning the plane left or right as Ernie directed him. It took immense courage to plough straight on into the inferno when all of your instincts told you to get away, to climb, to turn, to dive, to do anything but fly straight ahead. Even after the bombs had been dropped Min still had to fly straight and level for a minute or so while Ernie took pictures of the bomb bursts below.

Finally we were able to turn sharply north and were soon clear of the area. All of the crew were safe and we were able to head for home. The track home was much the same as the track out except we turned partway up the North Sea leg to head for Lincoln, passing the mouth of the Wash on the way. Over the North Sea, Ernie checked for hang-ups, but all of the bomb load had been dropped. At Lincoln there was a short leg to the Humber River and then into base where we landed at 1229. We had been airborne for four hours and fifty minutes and had flown 1,024 air miles.

Once back at base, Min had the ground crew check the aircraft for damage and, surprisingly enough, they found only one pinhole in a bomb bay door. The squadron had put up twenty-two planes and all carried out the assignment and returned safely to base. Of the entire raiding force, three bombers were lost to anti-aircraft fire and Min had seen two of them go down.

At this point in the war, the Allies had crossed the Rhine and shortly thereafter the army group of Field Marshall Model was bottled up in the Ruhr and a quarter of a million men cut off from escape. Model committed suicide rather than join his men in captivity.

On thinking back it is obvious that luck played a huge part in escaping injury in the circumstances we had experienced. The Germans were simply blanketing the sky and, in this instance, they had a lot of guns and they had the correct height at which to have the shells explode. Your plane flying through all the explosions was buffeted by bursts all around, on either side, above and below. You were flying at a speed of 217 knots, or about 107 yards a second. Perhaps only half a second meant the difference from flying through a puff of smoke and actually being in the wrong spot when the shell burst. Minute differences in your track resulted in the same hit-and-miss arrangement. You were probably just as safe flying straight and level as you would have been by taking evasive action of some sort. The difference, of course, was that all your instincts told you to do the latter while you had to follow the former course. In these circumstances the pilots had to have nerves of steel—and Min was no exception.

This episode certainly captured Min's attention, as attested to by his personal notes:

> Ops - Münster - The town, troops and communications. Height - 17,000. Load - one 2,000 lb. cookie plus 11 incendiary clusters - 8,250 lbs. 250 aircraft. Target 10:19.5. Object was to wipe out the town for army co-op.
>
> Flak moderately heavy and accurate. Saw one kite go down in flames, explode, and fall to the ground in sections just before target. Another Hali spinning, regaining partial control, and finally after about two minutes full control but losing height fast. No parachutes from either one.
>
> The most accurate flak we have seen so far. Damn near got hit on the way in. Felt the thud of one and concussion of another. I was sweating by the time we cleared out.
>
> Gaggle formation. Visibility 15 to 20 miles. Bang on prang. Master Bomber control. Saw fields strewn with gliders on the way out - Monty's new bridgehead over the Rhine.
>
> We had heavy fighter support all the way over Jerry land.

From my small window I did not see the aircraft go down so missed that. I have to disagree with Min's assessment of the anti-aircraft fire. I thought it was very heavy! Min could not of course have a hand on his parachute but I expect he gripped the control column hard enough to leave the impressions of his fingers on it! As a matter of interest his sweating took place while the temperature was minus forty degrees F!

F/L Forsdyke of our C Flight had looked at my logs of previous trips before and, apart from the odd suggestion or mild criticism, had not said too much. However, he really jumped on this effort with both feet. I am sure it was because he did not want me to become complacent in my duties and perhaps get myself and my crew into trouble.

There were twenty-eight questions and exclamation marks throughout the log. In one spot he said, "Don't be lazy. Enter some information occasionally!!!" The three exclamation points are his. On the last page he wrote, "Always treat a daylight gaggle as a night operation navigationally—it's good practice—to put it bluntly don't be lazy!!!!" Note there were four exclamation marks this time.

Once I had calculated a correct wind speed and direction and we were proceeding bang on track, I did slacken off somewhat. There seemed little point in rehashing what was obviously working. I had to agree with Forsdyke, much as I did not want to, that I had indeed been lazy. Still, we had made it back in one piece and nothing he wrote on my log could detract from that fact, especially after the type of run we had had over the target.

* * *

We were on our way home. We had completed our bombing mission over Münster, flown back across Belgium and France, and were now on the long leg taking us north over the North Sea to our base in Yorkshire. I had obtained a couple of GEE fixes showing us on track and we had a straight run ahead of us for an hour.

Since we had been over the target I had known this moment was coming, but youth, a strong bladder, and more importantly certain muscles, had been called on to perform above and beyond the call of duty. They now signalled they could do no more. I had to go to the bathroom!

The Halifax aircraft had a toilet located near the tail of the plane. It was known as a Burton after the man who designed it. This was the first, last and only time I had needed to use it, and one such experience was more than enough.

I switched on my intercom and advised the pilot I was going to use the toilet. "Roger," came his reply. I made sure my navigational instruments were safely stowed and disconnected my intercom. As we were flying over 8,000 we were using oxygen and I had to shut off the supply and also disconnect the narrow hose running to my facemask. I left both the intercom wire and oxygen tube dangling from my facemask, as I would have need of them shortly. Then my journey began.

My station toward the nose of the aircraft was lower than the pilot. In fact when I was seated at my table, my head was level with his feet on the rudder pedals. His work finished for the day, the bomb-aimer sat in the co-pilot's seat beside the pilot. There was one giant step, up which I had to hoist myself to get to their level. Two steps would have been nice, but the designer of the aircraft had decreed one—and a large one it was, especially with all the gear you were wearing. Once I had gotten up the step I had to squeeze between the pilot and bomb-aimer, making sure I did not snag my clothing or other things hanging from me.

Next came the wireless operator to pass, and this was not too bad. Next came the engineer. He raised the jump seat on which he perched and stood up to let me pass. He was a young, irreverent Scot and I could have sworn that underneath his oxygen mask he was grinning and humming, "Passengers will please refrain from flushing toilets while the train is standing in the station . . ." one of his favourite bawdy songs. Finally after carefully skirting the mid-upper gunner, there it was in all its glory.

A walled-in bathroom it was not. Simply a square, box-like structure out in the open with a lid to be lifted, under which was a seat. The seat was fixed and could not be raised, as no one in his right mind would have stood to do anything, what with the possibility of turbulence. Intercom and oxygen again plugged in, I informed the pilot where I was. He probably knew, as he would have trimmed the aircraft to allow for my weight shifting from the front to the back of the plane. Again I heard one word: "Roger."

Now began the laborious task of ridding myself of clothing. First I had to take off the parachute harness. Straps over my shoulders and coming up from between my legs met at a buckle in my mid-section. I tried to press on this to release the straps, but it was going to take more than a simple push. I had to give the buckle a sharp blow with my fist and that almost caused a catastrophe, as my weakening retentive muscles almost gave way. I laid the harness beside me on the floor. At that point I wished we wore bomber jackets like the Americans, but no, we had one-piece flying suits that were worn over our battledress. Unzipping the zipper from throat to crotch, I then sweated and heaved to extricate my arms and pushed the suit down around my ankles. Then it was easier to unbuckle my belt and push my trousers down to join the flying suit in a great bulky bundle below my knees. Finally, down went my underwear, which I knew to be clean, and which I hoped stayed that way. (Before each op we were required to take a shower. I don't think this was to impress the Germans if you were shot down, but rather to avoid getting dirt in wounds. Since you had taken a shower, clean underwear seemed natural.) At last I was ready to seat myself and proceed with the task at hand. You have no idea the relief I felt!

Sitting on the toilet with your posterior bare, you felt most vulnerable. It was stupid to think that your trousers and flying suit offered any protection whatsoever against bullets, shells and anti-aircraft fire but in your mind they did. Once you had reversed the undressing procedure by getting dressed, you again felt secure against harm from below.

There was a lever at the side of the Burton that you pulled to flush. I did not want to know, and I never asked, if there was a retaining tank attended to by the long-suffering ground crew, or if the contents simply fell to earth like "gentle rain from heaven."

You again worked your way around the other members of the crew, getting down the huge step—which was easier than getting up—and, once seated at your station and all plugged in once more, you told the pilot you were back at work. Back came the noncommittal "Roger." The skipper was a man of few words! It was fortunate that *he* never had to make the trip back to the Burton. After all, who would have flown the plane?

When you were flying ops, death was a distinct possibility, but aircrew would not even consider this fact. They would not admit it even if someone on the squadron were killed. They simply made believe that he was just not in his usual place. He wasn't in his billet, the mess or anywhere around; he was simply away somewhere. To explain his absence they said "he went for a shit." Over time, aircrew began to use the euphemism "he went for a Burton," which phrase was certainly more acceptable, especially in mixed company. I wonder how many other airmen, like myself, had gone for a Burton and returned from the ordeal?

* * *

After the raid on Münster our crew was given a short leave, and after eight operational flights in fifteen days we were glad to take it. As per usual I took the train down to my Aunt's in Trowbridge. While I was there curiosity got the better of them and my aunt asked what I had been doing. It had been drummed into us so often that we were not to tell anyone about squadron operations, all I could bring myself to say was, "I guess you read about the recent 1,000 plane raids. Well—!" To their credit they asked no more. Even the civilian population had been trained in secrecy and they knew that the less they knew, the less they could inadvertently tell others.

During the war the British people were still allowed to have coal fireplaces; as a result this, together with industrial smoke and automobile fumes, resulted in the worst possible smog in the cities. When a naturally occurring fog came along, the combination settled over the landscape like a blanket and visibility was restricted to just a few feet.

There was a postbox at the corner of my aunt's street on the same side as her house. To get to it, you simply had to walk along a sidewalk for perhaps 100 feet and partway round a gentle curve. Once the fog was so thick she got lost going that short distance!

On this leave you could not see the houses on the other side of the street that were perhaps just fifty feet away. Beryl and I went to the movies one night and we found our way downtown by going from street lamp to street lamp. When the glow from one was disappearing you could just pick up the light from the next; and so you went until you reached the theatre. The bad weather persisted and I received a couple of telegrams from the station extending my leave a couple of days each time. What lovely surprises they were.

A lot of things were rationed in England during the war and you received coupons that you could use for your allotment of the item. We received coupons for clothing, but our uniforms were relatively new and we hardly used them. As the coupons were not in any way designated for our own use I took them to my aunt's and gave them to that family. I went out with Aunt Rose and Beryl to a shop, where Beryl bought a new dress using some of the coupons. It was the first new dress she had had since the war began in 1939, five years before. The expression on her face was priceless as she tried it on and wore it that evening for Michael. At times we just did not understand what the people in Britain had been going through, but moments like this helped us a little bit to understand better.

Michael lived with his mother, and I was taken to see her once. She was an elderly lady of the "old school" and was a staunch advocate of the British Empire. During the conversation I was referred to as a Colonial, and Canada as a distant colony, which she saw as being far beneath England. As it turned out, having been born in England I was at the time English; and in Canada I was a landed immigrant—as I found out well after the war when I applied for a Canadian passport!

*   *   *

People born in Wiltshire were called "Moonrakers." A story, perhaps apocryphal, was told that the people, to escape paying taxes on the liquor they had made, sank the barrels of whisky in a river whenever the tax collector came around. Once the inspector sneaked back to find the people fishing the barrels out of the water with a long rake. It was a moonlit night and the moon's reflection was clearly shining on the water. It was explained that they were raking the river for the moon! I have always enjoyed the thought of being a Moonraker, which seemed to me to have a certain panache. I wish I had thought of telling Michael's mother that I was a Moonraker, just like her.

*   *   *

When you enlisted in the air force there were three branches from which you could choose: aircrew, ground crew and the office staff. Everyone had their own reasons for picking the branch in which they wished to serve. Obviously aircrew was the most hazardous and so it was the airmen who flew on operations who received all the attention in the press and seemed to be the most glamorous. We who were in that branch felt we were a cut above the other two branches.

However, the office work had to be done by someone. On squadron, airmen who had finished tours or a number of tours were put in charge of the trades in a flight with which they were familiar. For example F/L Forsdyke, the navigation officer for C flight, had been a navigator. These men were assisted by clerks, typists, and so on; but they themselves had earned the right to instruct, and to have a rest from flying on combat missions.

The unsung heroes of squadron were the members of the ground crew. These men, mostly sergeants or lower, worked long hours and without fanfare or glory; yet they saved many, many lives. I am afraid to say we paid them little attention, although I believe Min had words with them on occasion. When we flew we took it for granted that the plane was airworthy; that our parachutes were in order if required; that when we turned on the oxygen there would be a good supply for every crew member; that when the engineer switched petrol tanks, this exercise would be carried out without mishap and that there would be no change in the rhythm of the engines; that the guns would operate and the ammunition would be in place; that the navigational instruments were all working perfectly; and that the bomb load was well in place and no hang-ups would occur. Of course none of these things would have gone so well if the ground crew had not done their work properly.

They were a dedicated lot and often waited at the field to make sure the aircraft for which they were responsible had returned, even though that meant long, tedious hours at the field. If the pilot told them about something he had noticed, they would check it out and let him know. After the Münster raid when there had been so much flak, Min asked the ground crew to check the aircraft for holes. Surprisingly enough they found only one pin-sized hole in the bomb bay doors; but they checked the whole plane over thoroughly.

I have read only one book of memories written by a member of ground crew and that chap arrived on squadron very late in the war and saw little service on an active station. It is a shame that their courage, dedication and contribution to the war effort have not been recognized as strongly as is warranted.

* * *

In mid-April of 1945, an Order of the Day was published on every bomber command station throughout the United Kingdom. It was from Sir Charles Portal, chief of the air staff, to Sir Arthur Harris, air chief marshal, and it said:

> The tasks given to the British and American strategic air forces in Europe were to disorganise and destroy the German military, industrial and economic systems and to afford direct support to our forces on land and sea. In the first of these tasks we are now at the point of having achieved our object . . . henceforth, the main task of the strategic air forces will be to afford direct support to the Allied armies in the land battle and to continue their offensive against the sea power of the enemy.[6]

---

[6] Ibid., p. 215

Chapter 10

On April 18th, Min's name again appeared on the duty roster. By this time we had the drill down pat and had no trouble in preparing for the flight. I think we were even getting used to the pre-flight meal of greasy bacon and fried eggs with bread and jam for dessert! The target this time was Heligoland, and twenty-eight planes from 158 Squadron were scheduled to take part. Heligoland is an island located in the North Sea about thirty miles west of the coast of Germany that juts up to join Denmark. It contained an airfield and naval installations. Almost 1,000 planes from a number of squadrons were to take part in the raid. This trip would be somewhat like the "sweepstakes" we had flown at Conversion Unit, as we would be flying east over the North Sea and back.

After the main briefing, I filled in the top portion of my log, pencilling in the forecast wind velocities and directions and the air temperatures at various heights. Following that section I filled in the orders—our takeoff time and the times we were supposed to be at turning points, as well as when we were to start and stop windowing. There was also an order to take a radar picture five miles from the target.

Finally I filled in the information concerning our route, which was to consist of fourteen legs. For each of these legs there were twelve figures to record. These included the time to start each leg, the required track, the wind velocity and direction, the course to be flown, the height to be flown, our true air speed, our dead-reckoning ground speed, the distance to run to the next leg, and the estimated time of arrival. Navigators had a lot of paperwork to do even before the plane ever left the ground!

Our aircraft was to be V–Victor, an old warhorse of a plane that had already returned from forty-nine operational flights. Some patches on the side of the plane covered the scars of antiaircraft fire.

Our takeoff time was supposed to be 1121, but for some reason it was 1132 when I recorded Airborne Base in my log. In the aircraft I had already checked the escape hatch, loaded the Very pistol and checked the various instruments at my station. (I was never quite sure why it was my job to load the Very pistol, and I was not happy

Halifax Mark III. This is V-Victor. We used this aircraft on the op to Heligoland. Note the bombs painted on the fuselage. Each bomb represents an operational flight. Patched up here and there, this kite was a veteran of fifty bombing missions. To the left, below the cockpit, the small, white square over the bombs is my little window. These planes looked huge to us, but today one of these would fit under one wing of a commercial jet!

W.R. Chorley, In Brave Company

handling a gun of any description.) After circling and gaining a height of 5,500 feet we set out on our first leg at 1158 on a course of 071 at an air speed of 168 and an estimated ground speed of 189 knots.

My first couple of GEE fixes showed that the wind direction was closer to north than anticipated and we were a few miles south of track. However, the next leg swung slightly to the north and after that turned slightly to the south, so I gave Min a course that would intersect the track that bore to the south and we reached that spot at 1229. From then on, having calculated a correct wind direction and speed, I was able to feed Min courses that kept us close to track for the remainder of the flight to the target.

Our route took us some sixty or seventy nautical miles north of Heligoland, at which point we turned almost due south to reach the target. Presumably this was to indicate to the enemy we were going after a target in northern Germany or even Denmark before disclosing what the real target was.

We had climbed to an altitude of 16,500 feet and it was not long before the island could be seen, as dense smoke was pouring upward from oil fires started by the bombardment. The island was not very wide and the bombers could only go in two—or at the most three—abreast if they were to drop their bomb loads on the island. We were slightly off to one side and we would have risked a collision if we had tried to muscle our way into the long stream of planes approaching the island. Accordingly Min flew past to one side of the island and completed a large circle that brought us back on a second approach, and this time we were able to fly right over the target. Our bombs were dropped at 1346, six minutes after our time of scheduled delivery.

As we passed the island for the first time we had a splendid view of the area. Our aircraft was fitted with H2S, and I swung the camera, which was mounted on a swivel, around and took a picture of the screen showing the whole island slightly off to one side. We had been told at the briefing that there were thirty-two antiaircraft guns on Heligoland; but by the time we arrived, some fifteen minutes after the raid started, only two were still firing and then only spasmodically. The attack on the island was totally devastating.

After a short dogleg, the route home was almost in a straight line and was quite uneventful. Of the 1,000 or so planes taking part in the raid only three were lost. Because of the dense smoke the master bomber at one stage of the raid called "Basement 14" in order to have bombs dropped from a lower level. Not everyone heard this command and at least one of the aircraft lost was the result of being struck by bombs falling from above! We did not hear this order and bombed from 16,500 feet, but our bomb-aimer had a clear view below the plane and no other aircraft crossed below us. Although all planes were supposed to be at the same height, some differences were bound to occur, and you could see some planes twenty or thirty feet higher than you and sometimes a little lower. On one of our flights a plane trying to turn somewhat sharply to get over the target drifted below us, but passed to one side before any harm was done.

We arrived back at base at 1535 and landed at 1559, having been in the air for four hours and twenty-seven minutes after flying 785 miles. The navigation officer, F/L Toogood, wrote "Average trip" on my log but still pointed out I had done only four compass checks! We did not know it at the time but this was to be our last operational flight. Our squadron participated in one further raid, a trip to the island of Wangerooge, but we were not called upon for that journey. All twenty-eight planes from 158 Squadron returned safely from Heligoland and all were successful in their bombing.

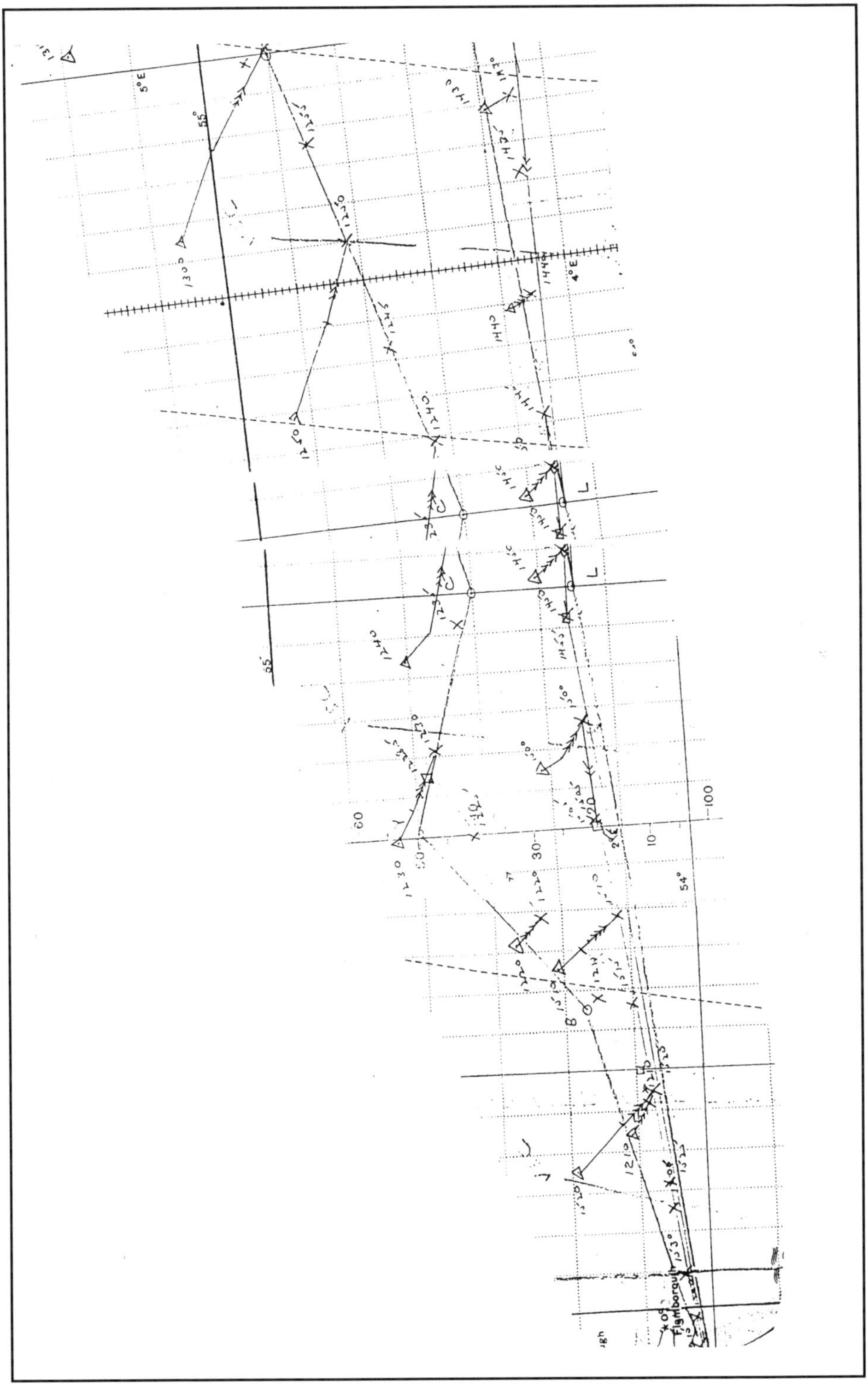

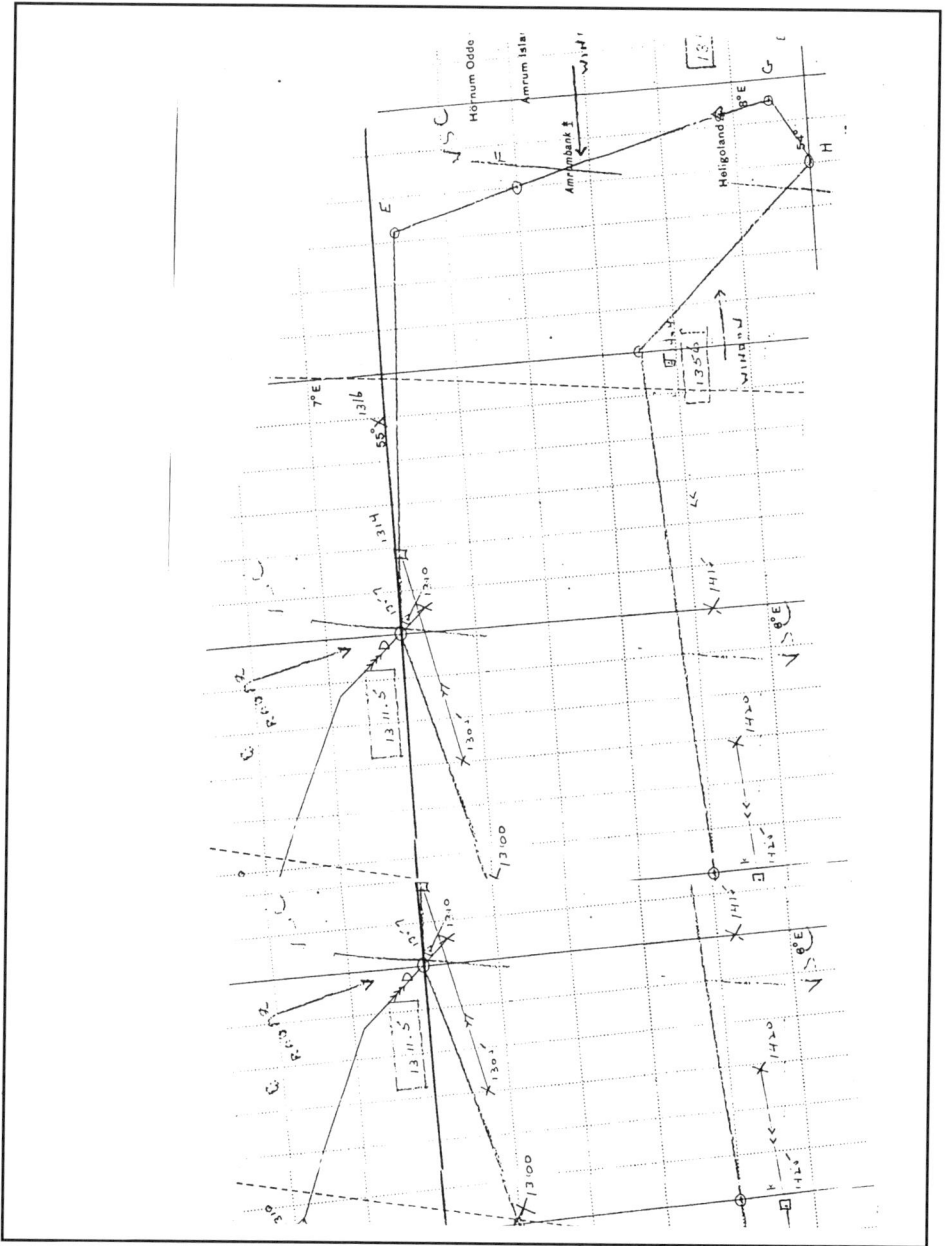

Chart: raid on Heligoland

Author

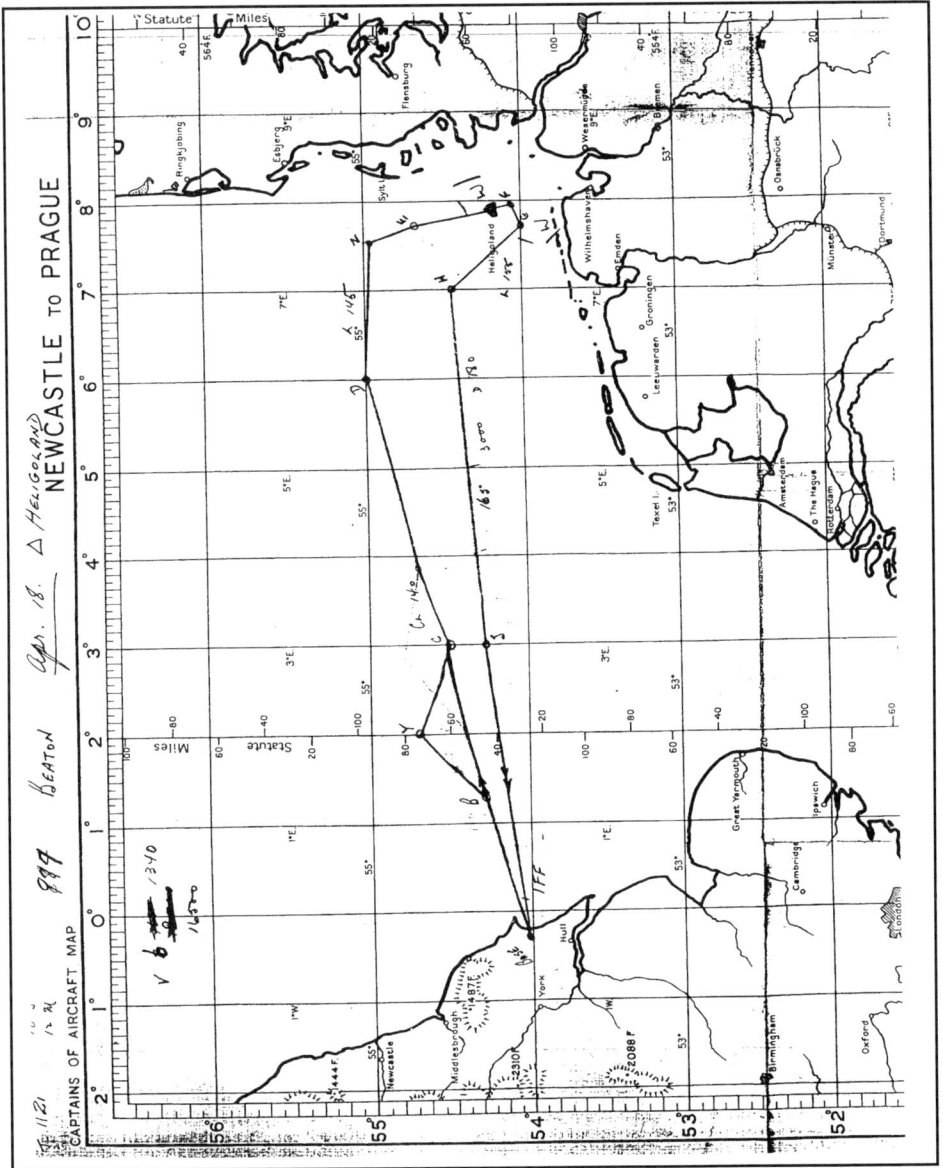

Min's map for Heligoland

Menno Bartsch

For some reason, Min went into quite a bit of detail with respect to this raid, as his personal journal shows:

> Load, 8 x 1,000 + 5 x 500 = 10,500 lbs. Height 16,500 feet. 977 bombers + Pathfinder Mosquitos + 10 squadrons of Spits + 12 squadrons of Mustangs. Target at 1346 hours. Object, to wipe the islands off the map and to destroy naval and air installations. Our aiming point was the town, stores, and billets.
>
> Weather ideal. Scattered patches of altostratus on route. 7/10ths stratocumulus in area and clear immediately above target.
>
> Master bomber controlled. Orbitted to the right once. Got a good look at the target. It was a helluva mess then, great billows of smoke drifting up and blowing downwind for miles. After that about 200 of us plastered what was left.
>
> We were expecting and were protected from Jerry "squirts" but saw none. Gunners saw one Hali go down with smoke from both inners.
>
> Remainder of trip uneventful. Flak almost negligible, only about half a dozen puffs. There were supposed to be 27 AA guns but most of them must have got it in the first wave.

* * *

There are two footnotes to this op. Many years later I was working with an Australian who had flown Spitfires. In comparing notes one day we discovered we had been over Heligoland at the same time as he had flown cover for the bombers. We had not seen any enemy fighters or our friendly Spitfires at the time. When we went back to our department we told one of the girls who worked with us and she said "It is more of a coincidence than you think, as my fiancée, a Spitfire pilot, was killed on that raid!"

Some forty years after the war, Min and his wife invited a German couple to their home whom they had recently met. During the after dinner conversation, the German fellow said he had been an anti-aircraft gunner on Heligoland when we had bombed the island. His story of leaping out of a bomb shelter to fire off one or two rounds and then diving into the shelter to wait for another slight lull in the bombing before he dashed out again was so funny that both Min and the German chap were howling with laughter. Their wives found it hard to believe: years before, they had both been intent on killing each other; but here they were, laughing at what had happened!

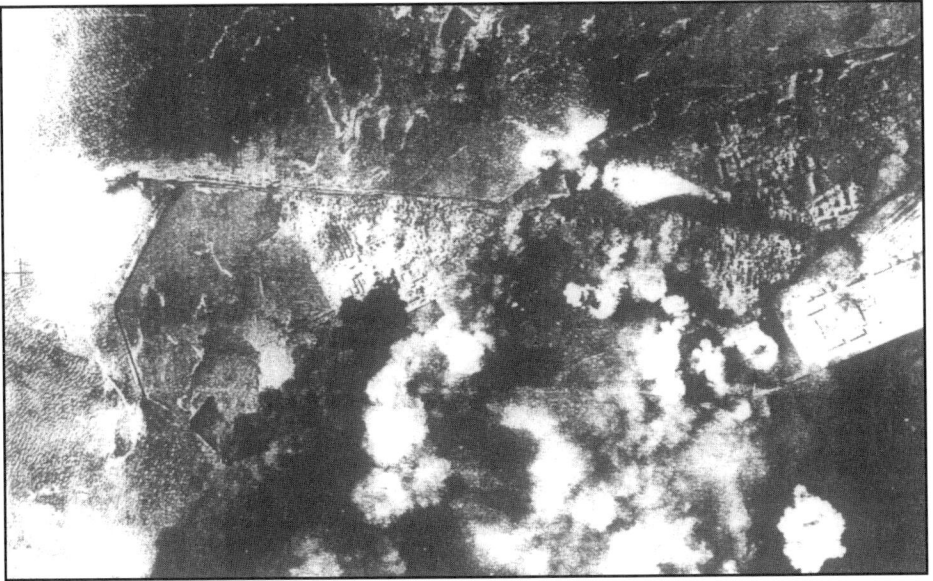

Aerial photograph of Heligoland taken on April 18, 1945 in the midst of the raid. It was taken from the aircraft *Friday the 13th*. A dense pall of smoke virtually covers the island. The burst from an anti-aircraft shell can be seen in the upper left-hand corner of the photo.

W.R. Chorley, In Brave Company

ODD JOBS

The war was over. No more wondering if you would be flying on an op. No more danger. There was a state of euphoria on the station. Through the latter part of April we whiled away the time on the station or went on short leaves. There was still some activity and Min did all he could to get us involved in any flying to be done. He hung around operations headquarters and volunteered us for anything that came up. To say that he loved to fly was an understatement! We did one trip of almost three hours ferrying an aircraft to a station in southern England. Then the station looked for someone to drop old bombs out in the North Sea and Min applied for this trip. The bombs had been in storage for some time in the buildup for the squadron's ops and, as bombs aged, the high explosives inside the casing tended to harden and become unstable.

We were given a latitude and longitude in the North Sea where we were to drop the bombs and off we went. Ernie tended to the bombing and I did the bit of navigation that was required, and we were soon at the designated spot. The bombs were not to be fused and it was assumed they would just hit the water and sink. We were not flying at a high level—perhaps 2,000 feet—when Ernie dropped the bombs. Obviously the stories about it being safe to handle these explosives were highly exaggerated, as they all exploded on impact, sending up great fountains of water. It was a good thing Min had kept us as high as he did.

We turned for home and, for a little horseplay, Min took the plane right down to the deck and we were just skimming the waves; in fact Ernie in the nose said his feet were getting wet. At that height the feeling of speed was tremendous and one we had not experienced before. I am not sure all of us liked it! A few miles offshore, Min pulled up and we climbed to several thousand feet. We learned later our sudden appearance on radar gave the operators on shore some concern.

Our plane was equipped with H2S and there were a dozen or so ships near the coast. They appeared quite clearly and separately on the screen and I did a count and checked with Min, who verified I had been accurate.

This was our last flight together as a crew. We had learned over a short period to trust the other members with our lives, and that built up a feeling of respect and friendship that went beyond normal relationships. We were not all close, but some special friends evolved. I guess my friendship with Menno Bartsch, my (shit-hot) pilot, meant the most to me, and that friendship has lasted for over fifty-seven years. It is safe to say that had it not been for Min's skills as pilot I would not be here, and this book would never have been written.

During our stint at 158 Squadron, the base had put up a total of 332 aircraft taking part in sixteen sorties. We had flown on only nine of these ops, during which time one plane failed to return. During the life of the station, from February 1942 to April 1945, 5,371 aircraft had been sent out from the squadron and 851 airmen had been killed—a terrible toll. Remember this was just one squadron in dozens of such stations.[7]

* * *

As the war in Europe ended, we were told that Canada intended to send an air force unit to the far east to fight against Japan. It was to be called "Tiger Force." We were given the opportunity to enlist for this force, which was to be set up back in Canada. Min and I decided to see the war through to the end and we signed up. We spoke to Stan Hare and Ernie Pollitt, the other Canadian members of our crew, but they wanted to get back to civilian life; so Min and I would have to start out with a new crew once we got back to Canada.

[7] Ibid., Appendix 8.

POSTED TO 158 SQDN. 5/3/4.

Time Carried Forward:— 157:35 / 100:00

Date 1944	Hour	Aircraft Type and No.	Pilot	Duty	Remarks (Including results of bombing, gunnery, exercises, etc.)	Flying Times Day	Night
MAR. 9	1655	Halifax III Z	F/O BARTSCH	NAV.	BOMBING X COUNTRY	4:30	
" 10	1600	Halifax III Z	F/O BARTSCH	NAV	BOMBING	1:20	
" 11	1200	Halifax III X	F/O BARTSCH	NAV	OPS. ESSEN	5:35	
" 12	1310	Halifax III X	F/O BARTSCH	NAV	OPS. DORTMUND	6:10	
" 13	1250	Halifax III X	F/O BARTSCH	NAV.	OPS. WUPPERTAL	5:45	
" 14	1720	Halifax III X	F/O BARTSCH	NAV	OPS. HOMBURG		6:15
" 15	1715	Halifax III X	F/O BARTSCH	NAV	OPS HAGEN		6:20
" 19	0050	Halifax III X	F/O BARTSCH	NAV.	OPS. WITTEN		6:35
" 21	0955	Halifax III Y	F/O BARTSCH	NAV	BOMBING	1:45	
" 24	0915	Halifax III X	F/O BARTSCH	NAV	OPS. GLADBECK	5:50	
" 25	0735	Halifax III X	F/L BARTSCH	NAV	OPS. MUNSTER	4:55	
		SUMMARY FOR MARCH 1945			TOTAL OPERATIONAL HRS.	28:15	19:10
					TRAINING HRS.	7:35	
					TOTAL	193:25	119:10

DATE

SIGNED

O.C. C FLIGHT

Total Time......

Logbook: 158 Squadron. The last page shows the totals of flying time for training and for operations. I had flown 279 hours and thirty minutes getting ready, and only fifty-one hours and fifty minutes fighting the war. But it seemed longer! (1 of 3)

Author

Time Carried Forward:— 193:25 / 119:10

Date 1945	Hour	Aircraft Type and No.	Pilot	Duty	Remarks (Including results of bombing, gunnery, exercises, etc.)	Day	Night
APRIL 15	1450	HALIFAX III U	F/O BARTSCH	NAV.	BOMBING F/AFF.	1:45	
" 18	1135	HALIFAX III V	F/O BARTSCH	NAV.	OPS. HELIGOLAND	4:25	
" 19	1250	HALIFAX III SB	F/O BARTSCH	NAV.	BOMBING F/AFF.	2:15	
" 20	1125	HALIFAX III V	F/O BARTSCH	NAV	BOMBING	1:30	
" 22	1125	HALIFAX VI X	F/O BARTSCH	NAV	BOMBING	1:15	
" 28	1130	HALIFAX III SB	F/L BARTSCH	NAV	BOMBING	2:05	
" 21	1025	HALIFAX III N	F/L LAWS	NAV	BOMBING	1:20	

SUMMARY FOR APRIL 1945

TOTAL OPERATIONAL HOURS
TRAINING HOURS
TOTAL TO DATE — 204:00 / 119:10

4:25
10:10

SIGNED .... O/C 'C' FLIGHT

(2 of 3)

Time Carried Forward:— 208:00 11:40

Date	Hour	Aircraft Type and No.	Pilot	Duty	Remarks (Including results of bombing, gunnery, exercises, etc.)	Day	Night
MAY 2	10:30	HALIFAX III T	F/O BARTSCH	NAV	FLYING FOULSHAM MANSTON	2:55	
" 4	10:35	HALIFAX III A	F/O BARTSCH	NAV	Jettison ... Sagon		1:15
			SUMMARY FOR MAY		TRAINING HOURS	4:10	
					TOTAL FOR 158 SQDN. OPS. TRNG. TOTAL	32:40 21:55 54:35	19:10 - 19:10
			TOTAL TO DATE		OPERATIONAL HOURS TRAINING HOURS TOTAL	32:40 179:30 212:10	19:10 /00:00 /00:00 /19:10

SIGNED .... F/L (RA) O/C 'C' FLIGHT

Total Time.....

(3 of 3)

We had one last leave in England, and needless to say I headed for my Aunt Rose's home in Trowbridge. When it was time to leave, my aunt and Dorothy saw me to the train station. As the train pulled in I said goodbye and gave my aunt a kiss on the cheek. She said, "Oh, for heaven's sake! Give the girl a kiss!" So I kissed Dorothy Boyle for the first time. My cousin Cecil, who married Dorothy after the war, always accused me of gallivanting about with his girlfriend while he was off fighting the war in the Middle East. Years later, when visiting another English cousin, she brought out a photograph of herself and Cecil in bathing suits relaxing on a beach just outside of Cairo. Cecil looked at the snap and said, "War is hell!"

We sailed home on the *Île de France*. This time instead of a small cabin I was in a huge room with a couple of hundred other men. The bunks were four deep and I was at the top! For one or two days during the voyage the seas became very rough, and one night the ship was leaning to one side so much I woke up just as I was about to fall out of bed. I liked to stand at the rail and watch the ocean roll by. One rough day, when I was standing about three decks above the water, the spray was coming that high from the bow wave and I could not stay long without getting drenched. Another day, flying fishes swam alongside for a few minutes. You could see them just below the surface skimming along and then suddenly one or two would give a great leap and fly through the air for several feet before diving smoothly back into the water.

There were lectures on board for those who wished to attend. One officer told us we would be returning to civilian life and we should perhaps tackle some different kind of work that had something to do with flying. He told us that northern Canada was just waiting for prospectors to unearth its riches. However, he said there was another way of looking for the buried treasures rather than prospecting on foot. Different kinds of ore under the ground put forth different minerals into the soil and the plants and trees growing over these deposits would be different depending on the type of ore. Having learned what vegetation was specific to each mineral, you could then fly over the forest and tell what sorts of deposits you were likely to find at a given spot. I don't know if anyone pursued such a vocation but it was an intriguing idea.

There was another lecturer on board. He was a civilian and I am not sure why he was allowed to give the lectures that he did. He was a member of the CCF party (Canadian Commonwealth Federation) and tried to convert us to that political group. He said we would soon be civilians again and we deserved to have the best government—which, he of course said, was his party. The old parties would drift along in their usual ruts and fresh air was needed in politics so that the workers would reap the benefits rather than the owners. One or two of our group were intrigued by this idea and one in particular began to try recruiting others.

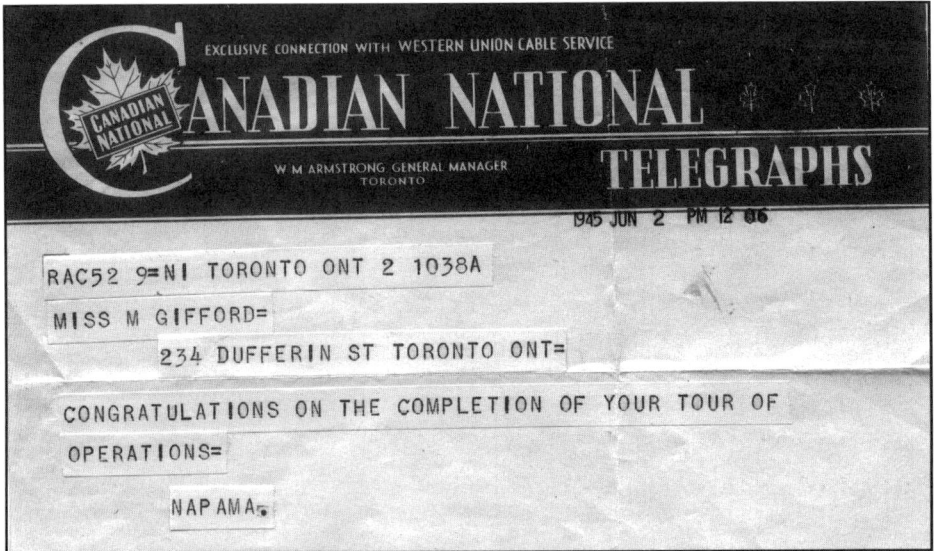

Telegram sent to Madelyn by her co-workers Naomi, Pat and Margerie.

Author

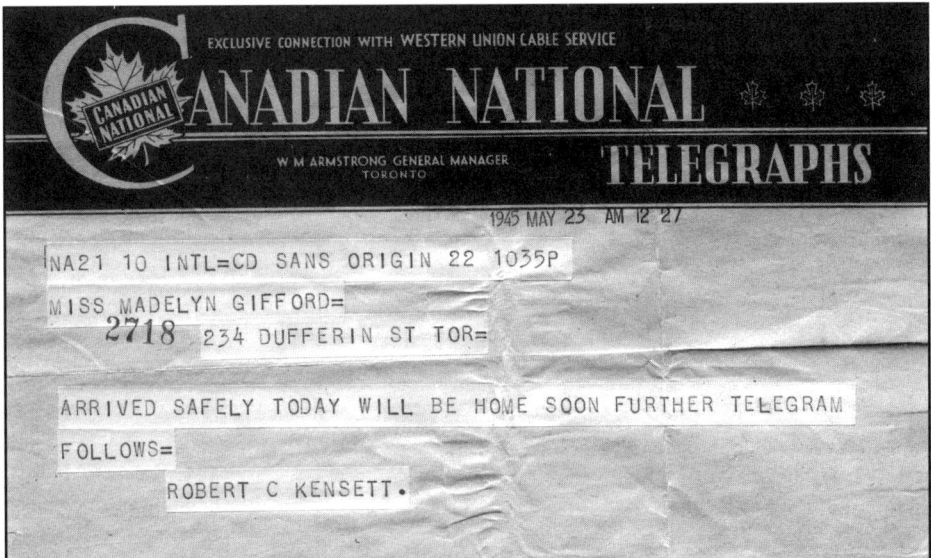

Telegram I sent Madelyn on my arrival in Canada.

Author

DARTMOUTH

On arriving in Canada we had two weeks' leave. My mother, sister and Madelyn met me at the train station. There were some friends waiting at our flat to welcome me home. After a very short while mother shooed everyone out and I was left alone with Madelyn. My, it was good to see her. We had a wonderful two weeks together before my leave was up and I was posted to Dartmouth. Min was posted there too, and there we spent the summer except for more intermittent leaves while waiting to get shipped out to Japan. I only had to get back to Toronto, but Min's home was in Port Alberni on Vancouver Island, so he was faced with long train trips each time he went home. He said that no matter how hard he tried he could only sleep twenty-two hours each day on the train!

The days were warm and I would often lie out on the grass and look up at the clouds coming in from the Atlantic. They were laden with moisture and on reaching land they billowed upward in huge cumulus clouds. The updrafts were so strong you could see the bumps in the clouds expanding and growing upward as the clouds moved inland. Somewhere in the distance there would be rain and thunderstorms, but over the station there was just blue sky.

Once in a while I took the ferry over to Halifax to see a movie, but most days I just loafed, wrote letters, and wondered what was coming next. One day the CO decided to have a parade and we were all taken out behind a hangar and lined up. The CO was obviously a career man, all for spit and polish. We were lined up and around the corner came the CO. When he saw our ragged ranks, many of us wearing hats with no wire in them so that they flopped over at the sides, some wearing white scarves, and all wearing bored expressions on our faces, he said, "Good God!" and disappeared. After a bit a junior officer decided there would be no parade and we were dismissed. We never had another one.

With the end of the war in the Pacific we received our conditional discharges. Conditional because we learned that once you had the king's commission you were the king's for life and could be called back into service at any time. I returned to my job at the bank. One day, soon after I started work, the manager of the branch took me to the bank's head office for lunch, where I ate with some of the bank's senior people. It is hard to say who was the more embarrassed as they tried to think of something to say to me, and I tried to keep up my end of the conversation. And so I settled again into civvy street.

Some years later I opened my trunk that I had kept in the cellar and took out my cap that I had worn so proudly. There was some mould on the brim and the insignia fell off onto the floor. Obviously my air force career was over.

This photo of Madelyn was taken when she was in her early sixties, a few years before she died.

Author

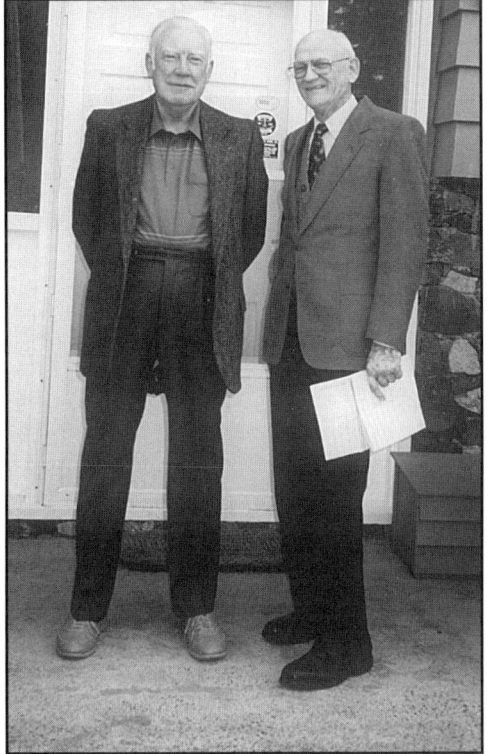

The author, on the left, and good friend Menno Bartsch in 1992. Neither would be in this photo were it not for the skills of the other.

Mrs. Olive Bartsch

EPILOGUE

In 1991 my beloved Madelyn passed away. In 1992 to get away from my surroundings and their ghosts I returned to England. I spent some time with my cousin Cecil Cleverley and his wife Dorothy who live in the picturesque village of Kemble in Gloucestershire. During my visit we drove to a town on the North Sea called Seahouses, where we stayed for a few days in a typical, comfortable, British hotel. It overlooked the harbour where one morning I saw a seal swim in from the sea hoping to find some refuse from the fishing boats that were berthed along the mole. When we started back to Kemble, Cecil was kind enough to drive down the coast to Bridlington, the seaside resort I had visited so often during the war. From there it was a short seven miles to the village of Lisset.

We drove slowly down the road and there was the gate to what had once been an airfield. We entered, and slowly passed one-storey structures that had been the guardhouse, dispersal huts, buildings where briefings had been conducted, and other places where we had waged our war so many years before.

The fields were once again farmland. A barely discernable track encircled what had once been the airfield. Cecil slowly drove around the perimeter allowing me a good look at the place. Only one paved portion remained of the cement runway, about fifty yards square, and a few pieces of farm machinery stood silently in one corner. A couple of the buildings were being used by the farmer for storage purposes, but the remainder were crumbling derelicts with windows broken, roofs caving in and walls disappearing behind suffocating vegetation. We stopped for a moment and a roughly dressed old gentleman came over and stood at the side of the car. I explained to him why we were there but I am not sure he understood. He muttered a few words but his Yorkshire accent was such that I could not understand him at all!

He slowly walked away and all was silent as I gazed across the fields. Before we drove off, leaving the memories behind, I closed my eyes and it took little thought to see and hear those great beasts, under a full bomb load, all 104 engines of twenty-six aircraft roaring, as one by one they staggered down the runway and lifted into the sky on yet another walk in the valley.

ABOUT THE AUTHOR

Robert Kensett was born in a pub owned by his grandfather in Wiltshire, England. He was brought to Canada at the age of three months. After three years of high school he had a forty-five-year career as a banker, starting as a pageboy and retiring as an assistant general manager. His banking career was interrupted by some three years in the RCAF in World War II as a navigator in Bomber Command.

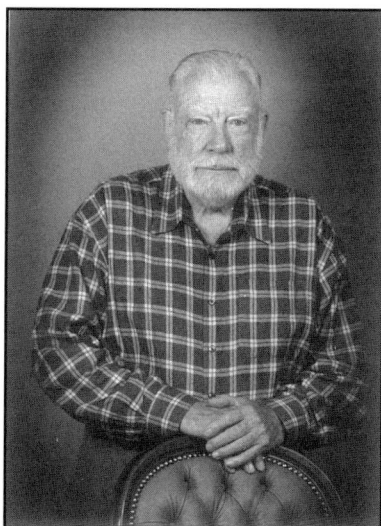

Married twice, he lost both wives to cancer. After retirement he turned to writing. In 1999 he self-published a book of poetry, and a second book of poetry, and a second book of poetry is in the works. Essays, anecdotes and some humorous articles have been published in the magazines of the Victoria Naturalist and Ulyssean societies, of which groups he is a member. He is presently working on a book about growing up on a farm.

An avid birdwatcher, he loves to travel, the most recent trip being to Africa. There he amazed his friends (and himself) by sleeping in a tent in Namibia while hyenas roamed the campground at night laughing hysterically!

Now seventy-eight, the author tells everyone he has to live into his nineties in order to finish all the projects on his plate!